Why
WHISTLE-BLOWERS
HESITATE

WHAT DO YOU DO WHEN THEY THREATEN
TO KICK THE WIND OUT OF YOU?

An Autobiography of a *Whistle-Blower*

Robert D. Durrett, Ed. D.

ISBN 978-1-64569-523-3 (paperback)
ISBN 978-1-64569-524-0 (digital)

Christian Faith Publishing, Inc.
832 Park Avenue
Meadville, PA 16335
www.christianfaithpublishing.com

All biblical references but one are taken from the Holy Bible, NIV 1971, 1978, 1984, and 2011, by Biblica, Inc.

Printed in the United States of America

DEDICATION

This book is dedicated to Carolyn, my best friend, companion and wife of 55 years. I am eternally grateful to you for praying for me and supporting me during my times of trial through an unlawful termination and praying me through chemo treatments after we were told my cancer was incurable. Thank you for hanging in there when I am sure my attitude was less than loving. Bless you for loving me back into God's kingdom with your loving kindness and continual invitation to come and be renewed. You taught me about faith through your examples and steadfast resolve. Thank you for our two wonderful kids; may they also be strengthened by your example. God bless you, my love.

Never has a man had better advocates than my lawyers, Thomas Stanton and Christopher Antcliff. Tom and Chris not only offered comfort and support, they protected my rights through all the twists and turns of the legal process. My heartfelt thanks!

A special thanks to my dear friend and author Sandi Browne who encouraged me to tell my story. To Carolyn Woodul, she and Jack traveled many miles just to encourage me to fight through my chemo treatments because of her own successful treatments. God bless you, Carolyn! You gave me the gift of hope.

To my four brothers and two sisters, I thank them for their examples of what it means to be faithful to family and friends. A special thanks to Brother Charlie, the lawyer, who joined me during a crucial deposition during my journey through my three year legal struggle. And a special thanks to Brother Tom for helping me keep my early family history straight.

To great friends in my Walk to Emmaus reunion groups and team members in Kairos Prison Ministry, as well as men in and out of prison, who prayed for me during my legal battles and chemo treatments. God Bless you all.

PREFACE

For almost twenty years I have hesitated to write about my personal experience as a whistle-blower. I was terminated for exercising what I believed to be my duty as a public employee. So I wondered, what good would it do to write about it now? Who cares about local political misdeeds? And, we have laws to protect whistle-blowers, so move on.

Each day as I have listened to the daily news I have become convinced that my story is merely a minute speck of what goes on in the larger public arena. Current news regarding whistle-blowers having their homes invaded by authorities and/or being fired by authorities has convinced me to write and share my experience. Also, at my age and my recent battle with incurable cancer made it crystal clear that it was now or never.

A short personal history, much of which I am not proud, is interwoven within the text only to emphasize that people do "grow-up," change and/or mature. I pray that elected officials at all levels of government will mature, honor their oath of office and faithfully serve the needs of their constituents with honor.

The political climate of these times has led me to believe that the general public needs to take a close look at what has happened and is happening in the public arena. I have thought maybe, just maybe, my story might raise public awareness and would encourage others to become more engaged and examine what our elected representatives are doing or not doing to protect their constituents.

Just because we have laws to protect whistle-blowers does not mean that the agencies charged to enforce the laws actually perform their assigned duties. My disappointment in the state agencies, which were supposed to support and protect whistle-blowers like me, is indescribable. In my case they were nowhere to be found.

In the following pages I have purposely avoided mentioning the name of the teacher named in the complaint because he was not involved in the process leading to my termination. I have tried to only focus on the issues and individuals involved in my unlawful termination.

The issues raised by the parents, in the complaint which I filed, may seem trivial to some; but these parents believed the teacher was misusing their children and not focusing on their education.

Being reared by parents who believed their children should follow the rules gave me the courage to stand up for the parents because I agreed that the actions of the teacher were an inappropriate abuse of power. I thank God that my belief was rewarded and I was vindicated.

CHAPTER 1

THE COMPLAINT

The whistle-blower complaint I filed generated an unexpected journey for me from June of 1999 through July of 2002. During this time, I began to wonder, *Where are the defenders of whistle-blowers hiding?* The Texas statute said I had not only a right to file a complaint but an implied duty. That same statute promised that complaints would be investigated fully and appropriate action taken. Oh, woe is me. I believed it.

The event that resulted in *this* whistle-blower getting a dose of the reality occurred on August 10, 1999. That was the day I arrived at my office and received a notice of my suspension and possible termination because I had refused my boss's demand to withdraw a complaint. I did not know how precarious my journey would be.

I will share below the grounds that I would later understand were the cause of my termination and the touchstone for my legal claim that I was subjected to retaliation for protected speech.

I had served as associate superintendent for human resources (HR) for the school district for almost ten years, handled hundreds of complaints arising out of a variety of circumstances, and recommended several suspensions as well as a couple of terminations. I was very familiar with the suspension and termination process.

My journey began when I filed a formal complaint with the Texas State Board for Educator Certification (SBEC) on June 30,

1999. The essence of the complaint was contained in two simple paragraphs:

> Students alleged that on or about Saturday, April 10, 1999, (the teacher) picked students up at Riverside High School, Ysleta Independent School District, El Paso, Texas, to campaign for contested seats on the District's Board of Trustees by distributing and posting campaign materials. The students had been offered 10 points on their six weeks' average if they would participate. The offer was made during school hours, in the classroom while (the teacher) was on duty. The students were not given an opportunity to choose which candidates they would work for. Some students did not even know who they were campaigning for until that Saturday. The District's investigation substantiates the students' allegations.
>
> The investigation also showed that the campaign activity was not part of any lesson plan or with any curricular purpose. (The teacher) belongs to an employee organization, which endorsed the candidates the students were recruited to support. I believe (the teacher) used his institutional and professional privileges for personal or partisan advantage.

The SBEC complaint process required that I notify my boss that I had filed a complaint. Apparently, my new boss, Dr. Vargas, disagreed with me; and he made sure I knew it. He demanded that I withdraw the complaint and expressed his displeasure with me in his written response which he sent to me by personal delivery.

When I received his letter suspending me, my thoughts turned to focusing on where my idea about filing a formal complaint with the SBEC had come from. Two thoughts quickly came to mind. One was that a group of parents were furious about what a teacher had done and they didn't think it was appropriate. And, second, I had become aware of a recent change in the Texas Administrative Code. This change was made on March 31, 1999, and *for the first time allowed me* (as an uncertified educator) to file a complaint regarding the conduct of employees which might violate the Texas Educators' Code of Ethics.

This change in the Administrative Code was very important to me. In the past I had been frustrated because I had been unable to get certified personnel to file code of ethics complaints even though they would complain to me. Now I no longer had to plead with the folks doing the complaining to take action; I could file a complaint myself. I guess you could say this turned out to be good news and bad news for me. It was good news that I could, and as it turned out it created some bad news for me that I did.

So how did a simple, lawful, two-paragraph complaint lead to my suspension and threat of termination? I actually believed there were laws protecting state employees like me when they filed whistle-blower complaints. So why should I worry? I had the state on my side I thought. I found out why I, and other whistle-blowers, should worry during the next couple of years.

My journey as a whistle-blower began to unfold very quickly after I filed the complaint.

CHAPTER 2

CHARACTER BUILDING TIME?

Was it something ingrained in my character that made me refuse my bosses' demand to withdraw the complaint? In reference to character, President Reagan once said:

> The character that takes command in moments of crucial choices has already been determined by a thousand other choices made earlier in *seemingly unimportant moments*. It has been determined by the day-to-day decisions when life seemed easy and crises far away—the decisions that piece by piece, bit by bit, developed habits of discipline or laziness, habits of self-sacrifice or self-indulgence, habits of duty and honor and integrity, or dishonor and shame. (Emphasis added)

Being suspended I had some time to ponder my circumstances. I began wondering why I had filed the complaint. *What in the world had possessed me to proceed with filing this complaint? Personally, I had nothing to gain and a good-paying job to lose.*

Could I identify the "seemingly unimportant moments" in my background which made me so stubborn? Was it the influences of my *family*, my *dad*, my *friends*, my *prior experiences*, my *faith*, or plain old personal *fear* of being a quitter when my integrity was challenged?

Maybe it was something which I picked up from my family during my early childhood while growing up in Portales, New Mexico.

It was interesting how some memories came flooding back as I pondered my early childhood experiences, especially now that I was suspended and had lots of time to ponder who I was and what got me into my current situation.

I was born in the dentist's office in Melrose, New Mexico, in 1939. My family had just moved from Tucumcari, New Mexico; and I was told that my dad opened a small garage there. I do not have any independent memories of those early years. I do have an old photo of the little rock house my dad built that we lived in. He must have done a good job because when I last drove by in the late 1980s, it was still standing. My dad's brother, Uncle Buster, also lived there. He was a New Mexico State Police officer and later joined the FBI. I do remember that Uncle Buster always carried two pearl-handled revolvers and when he came to visit I always begged to see them. I was so proud that I had an uncle who was an FBI agent.

As the sixth of seven children and the youngest of the five boys, I learned to be independent at an early age. I was only two years old when WWII broke out and my family moved from Melrose, New Mexico, to Oakland, California.

My early memories of Oakland are standing outside our government-operated apartment building watching long lines of tanks moving toward the shipyards, hearing the rumble, and feeling the vibrations under my feet. My little sister was born in Oakland on December 30, 1943. Apparently seven kids were too many for one family in government housing; so my parents sent me to Portales, New Mexico, to live with my grandparents. The rest of the family followed after the war was over. Looking back, it was fun growing up in Portales.

My first real memories of the Portales area are after the family moved back to New Mexico. I grew up watching my dad try his hand at dryland farming as a share cropper in the sand hills of Roosevelt County, New Mexico. The only photo I have of that time is one made on Christmas Day of 1947 showing me and my next older brother, Jerry, kneeling with the wonderful presents we received that year. Our only gifts were small cattle trucks. They were wonderful because these trucks were made for us by two of our older brothers, Tom and Charlie, in shop class at high school. The photo also shows a rocking chair which was for my little sister, Ruth; and I don't know where it came from, but it was very special because it was "store-bought."

Other poignant memories came flooding back after I began searching my memories for events in my past, especially when I began looking at old photos. Because I had been sent to Portales to live with my grandparents during the war, I began elementary school at Eastward Elementary. I lived what seemed to me to be ten miles from school but was actually only a mile or so. The Harts were our neighbors. David Hart was my age, and we became best friends. We walked to school together each day.

My first attempt at first grade was less than stellar. It seemed that I could not stop talking. To quiet me down my teacher, Ms. Lillian, taped my mouth shut and hit my hand with her ruler. It was not a good incentive for me to want to go to school. As a matter of fact, I did not like school at all. It was an easy decision when David and I decided to play hooky. An older student, named Bobby as I recall, heard us talking about skipping school; and he suggested that we go to the Sunken Garden in the City Park just two blocks past the school. He said he would come and get us when school was out. Well, we didn't need to wait on Bobby to come and get us; we were missed at school. When Mrs. Randall, the truant officer, went to our homes to find out why we were not in school, the hunt was on. Apparently, it didn't take long for them to locate us in the Sunken Garden. We had been talking to the fellow who was the caretaker of the park; so, when Mrs. Randall came looking for us, he quickly informed her that he had been talking to two boys playing in the Sunken Garden. Apparently, we were not very good at hiding.

My folks could not believe I had played hooky. I was in deep trouble, and I just knew I was in for a whipping with the razor strap. However, when I told my folks that I did not like school because I did not like my hands being hit or tape being put on my mouth, their attitudes quickly changed. I don't know what went on in the principal's office. I just know that I did not get a whipping at home and the ruler-thumping and mouth-taping stopped. However, that did not seem to make a difference in my educational process because I did not successfully complete the first grade.

That series of events must have made an impression on me because I did successfully complete the first grade the second time around. The reason might have been that I did have a new teacher for my second attempt. And, much to my surprise and much, much later, Ms. Lillian reentered my life as an ardent supporter. There will be more on that later.

During my years in elementary school, we moved frequently. I attended all three of the local elementary schools. When we moved to Lime Street, I attended the third and fourth grades at Lindsey Grade School which was only four plowed fields away. The principal was called Uncle Arbow, and he was a very strict disciplinarian. The rumor was that if you crossed him he would whip you with a piece of black garden hose he kept in his office. I never received any whippings from him. I guess I feared that ole hose, so I made sure I followed the rules.

Lindsey was named after Governor Lindsey, and I liked going to that school. It had indoor plumbing! So I always tried to go to the bathroom before coming home. I planned ahead during bad weather and during the winter so I would not have to use our "outhouse" when I got home.

I do recall walking to Lindsey one snowy winter morning when the sun was very bright. I never made it to school that day. They came looking for me just like they did when I played hooky in the first grade. When they found me, I was wondering around in one of the plowed fields all wet and muddy. The bright sun shining on the snow had temporarily blinded me. I was sicker than a skunk and could not see anything for several hours.

From Lime Street we moved to State Street. Boy, oh boy, it was great! We finally had electricity and our own indoor toilet—no more running out the back door through the mud or snow to the "two-ho-ler" outhouse. And with electricity the kerosene lanterns were history. We were in "hog heaven," as my mom used to say.

What I do remember about State Street is that I could not figure out what made the light bulbs work. You pulled a string, and the light came on. My curiosity finally got the best of me. I turned on the light, climbed up on a counter in the bathroom, reached out as far as I could reach, and barely reached the bulb. It was dangling down from the ceiling on the electrical cord. I finally got the bulb unscrewed. But I could not hold the socket and put my finger in it at the same time. So I jumped off of the sink several times trying to stick my finger in the socket to see what was in there. Fortunately, I was unsuccessful. When I told my mom about my experiment, I thought she was going to faint.

Then there's learning ethics from a brother. That might not have been the best way! You know the Bible tells us that even Cain and Abel had some issues (Genesis 4:8).

Perhaps my family's influence on being honest and treating folks the way you wished to be treated might have helped me push for a little honesty within myself, or perhaps not. I recall one occasion during my junior high school days when I was ill and missed a day of school. The next morning my mom prepared a note for me to take to school explaining my absence. As I was walking toward the school, my older brother Jerry came running after me, shouting for me to stop and wait because he needed to talk to me. To my surprise, I learned he had been writing his own excuses when he decided to play hooky. He took the note my mom had written for me and replaced it with another one he had written. He was concerned that the truant officer might recognize the difference between Mom's handwriting on my note and the excuses he had previously written and he was going to write for himself in the future to take to school. I did not even think about what would happen after he graduated and I had to take one of Mom's notes.

My dad was a unique individual. He left me with a legacy of doing the right thing (as it turned out I was a little slow in catching on). He moved the family to Oakland, California, so he could work in the naval shipyards during WWII. He helped to build Liberty ships for the Navy. Dad was a "qualified American Bureau of Shipping welder for flat, vertical, and overhead welds." He worked as a welder at Richmond, California, Shipyard #1. He could weld anything! As a matter of fact, I believed he could fix anything. He never stood still, and he could not stand it if he caught one of us boys just standing around. If there was work to be done, we had better be working or looking for something to do.

The family tells the story of Dad's building a swing in the front yard of that housing project where the family was living. The "government man" came to tell him to take it down. As the story was told to me, it was a short and heated exchange of words; but the swing stayed in place because Dad knew the kids needed a place to play. My dad always told us that if we followed the rules, we wouldn't get into trouble. Apparently, he did not always "strictly" follow the rules. I guess I got some of my stubbornness from him. It is another small part of the legacy he left me.

I knew that my dad had not progressed past the third grade, but he valued education. Because he got his education in the school of hard knocks, he wanted something better for all of his kids; and that was why he moved the family to Portales, New Mexico, after the war.

Portales is a small rural farming community in eastern New Mexico. One great advantage was that it was also the home of Eastern New Mexico College (ENMC). The college was one of the major reasons Dad moved the family to Portales. The college later became Eastern New Mexico University (ENMU). His dream was for all of his kids to get a college education. And his dream almost came true. Out of his seven kids, the five boys received a combined eleven college degrees. Three became school teachers and/or educational administrators, one an attorney, and one a geophysicist. My older sister never attended college. She eloped and got married to her high school sweetheart when he returned home on leave from WWII. She was a very dedicated mom to her five kids. My younger sis attended ENMU but did not graduate. She became a certified legal assistant. I believe Dad was very proud of all of us.

I am positive every member of my family knew and acknowledged that Dad was a smarter and wiser man than any of us. His advice to us to follow the rules served us well (when we did). We were all very proud of him.

Eastern New Mexico College, the reason Dad moved our family to Portales. Now his kids could be at home and go to college.

Durrett Grandparents

Christmas day 1949 Jerry on the left with truck number 1, and Bob on the right with truck number 2. Our Christmas presents were made by our older brothers Charlie and Tom. Ruth's "store bought" rocking chair in the middle.

Family photo in Melrose before leaving for California where younger sister Ruth was born in 1943. Top row, Dorothy, Ed, Charlie. Middle row, Tom and mom. Bottom row, me and Jerry.

Dad with his boys. Left to right, Charlie,
Bob, Dad, Ed, Tom and Jerry.

Me and all of my siblings. Left to right, Ruth,
Bob, Jerry, Tom, Charlie, Dorothy and Ed.

Dad could fix anything. Rebuilding an engine in the dirt.

The 55-gallon barrel is the one Dad had cut in half so
we could move from the # 2 washtub into a "larger" tub.
Dad made everyone help, grandson Jim Durrett and me washing
car parts in our old bath tub (now we had in-door plumbing).

CHAPTER 3

What Were My Boss's Rules? Or How Did My Previous Actions Influence the Board?

I knew how to follow the rules because I had been a policy wonk throughout most of my career as an administrator. Some of my stubbornness must have come because I had been working with various policies, rules, and regulations for many years. Also my naivety and my upbringing had led me to believe that following the rules was the best policy. As a first grader, it had saved me from a spanking after playing hooky when I told the truth. Also, following policy and state regulations was what I had done in previous positions and was what I was good at and what I was hired to do, I thought.

So I had to ask myself, "*Why*? Why would my boss insist that I withdraw my complaint? Why would filing a legal whistle-blower complaint with a state agency draw such a quick and drastic response? After all I was just doing my job, right?" I was kind of slow in fully understanding the totality of my situation. One question for me was: Why not just withdraw it and move on?

Being a slow learner must be part of my psyche. I had received a lesson regarding following the rules earlier in my professional career. I was promoted and transferred from Denver, Colorado, to Houston, Texas. When I arrived at my new assignment as credit manager of a new Woolco Department Store, I was able to quickly set up the credit department and layaway area. Once I completed my tasks, I started looking for something else to occupy my time just as my dad had taught me. When I worked on road jobs with him, he did not like me to just stand around. He would tell me to find something to do and get it done. Well, I noticed that the shelving on the sales floor was going up very slowly. Since I needed something to do, I grabbed a hammer and started putting some shelving together. After about ten or fifteen minutes, I heard someone "blowing a whistle." I wondered what in the world was going on, so I stopped hammering and looked around.

Everyone I could see had stopped working.

All of a sudden, the store manager, Tom, came rushing over and asked me what in the world I was doing working on shelving. When I told him I was just trying to help out, he called me something like "stupid" with a few adjectives attached as he explained that the union foreman had pulled all the construction crews off of the job because of me. Needless to say, I spent the next several days doing nothing. All I could do was wait for the construction crew to finish and the store to open. Because of my dad's work ethic, I wondered what he would have said for my getting paid for doing nothing.

Looking back, it now seems that my role in the district was kind of like working in that Woolco store environment: Get out of line, and they "blow the whistle" on you. Because of what I had heard about the political climate in the district during the several years prior to my arrival and my thirty years of experience in the field of personnel management, I was not completely surprised at my predicament. But I still continued to wonder *why* me. *Why* now? What did I do wrong? It was not "my" complaint! My reason for filing a complaint was based solely on the allegations of misconduct lodged by parents against a teacher. So what was the nexus between my filing a whistle-blower complaint and my suspension and threat of termination?

I began to think about the history I had heard about and the circumstances of this large border town school district. When I arrived in the district, the Texas Department of Education had classified it as a "low-performing district." Consequently, there were many challenging issues facing the administration. It was the seventh largest school district in Texas with over fifty thousand students, three thousand-plus teachers, four thousand-plus support employees, and a bus fleet of three hundred-plus buses. Because of the large number of employees, it seemed that personnel-related issues were always popping up. While this parental complaint was kind of unique, I looked at it as just another personnel issue which needed to be handled.

So if it was just another personnel issue and I was following policy, what was the big deal? What was unique about this complaint? The SBEC had rules and regulations. The Texas Administrative Code was in place, and the board had a policy regarding how to handle these types of issues. Board policy was to appoint an independent review committee to investigate all allegations of misconduct. They were to investigate; prepare findings and conclusions; determine what action, if any, was called for; and make a recommendation through me (the associate superintendent for human resources) to the superintendent. I could either concur or not concur with the review committee. If I did not concur, I could either request further investigation by the committee or pass it on to the superintendent with or without a recommendation. The superintendent could concur or not and forward it to the board. I was very familiar with the process, because during my employment in the district, it had been my responsibility to oversee employee misconduct investigations. This process was well established; and the review committee had completed reviewing the issues, which had been raised by the parents, when I forwarded the parents' complaint to the SBEC.

In my opinion, this was a process that did not endear me to either of the two teacher organizations operating in the district or to some administrators for that matter. Also, during my tenure, I had made several operational changes and policy interpretations which the teacher organizations and some administrators did not approve. For example, on June 28, 1993, I gave one of my first controversial recommendations which directly affected both of the teacher organizations. It was in response to a consultation proposal made to the board by one of the teacher organizations. It was a proposal to continue a long-standing arrangement in which a teacher was assigned to halftime teaching duties but receiving full pay. The teacher was being paid from public funds for representing the organizations halftime. My conclusion was that this arrangement was a gift of public funds which I believed to be an illegal use of those funds. My recommendation was to deny the request and discontinue the practice. It was accepted and approved by the board, much to the dismay of the organization involved.

These teacher organizations were typically very active during school board elections. It might have been that recommendation which was the impetus for the organizations to ramp up their electioneering activities to change the board. Could their displeasure with my decisions, recommendations, and/or pursuit of misconduct allegations against teachers (especially this complaint) and their influence with the board be the nexus? I could not be sure.

Another example was an operational change I made to the substitute call center which impacted teachers. When I arrived at the district, the substitute call center utilized four employees. They came to work at 4:00 a.m. to receive calls from employees calling in ill or needing a substitute teacher for other reasons such as professional development training. After each call, they in turn began calling substitutes and assigning them to fill the open positions. This approach seemed to create some confusion each day because some teaching positions would not be filled before the school day began. Of course, each unfilled position created ill-feelings among principals, teachers, and the human resources division. After dealing with the situation for a full year, I installed a computerized substitute call system. This system only required one employee to operate. Consequently, three employees were transferred to open positions in the district; and their positions were eliminated from the call center budget.

The computerized system allowed for employees to call in at any time to report the reason and when and how long they would need a substitute. For example, when they called in sick for a day, the computer automatically began calling a substitute.

When a teacher was scheduled for a conference, the teacher could schedule his or her substitute for that period in advance of his or her absence. If the teacher had a particular substitute who had done a good job in the past, he or she could request that individual to be his or her substitute. Because of the high usage of sick leave, a daily report of usage was prepared and reviewed.

On one occasion, the leader of one of the teacher organizations scheduled herself to be sick four months in advance of when she was to be "sick." This was discovered in reviewing our daily report. I thought she had probably miscoded her request and would correct that entry before the date in question. However, during a review of the usage on the date in question, she was indeed absent. That day, it was learned she was attending her teacher organization's annual conference in Austin. Because the conference was scheduled for several days, I dispatched one of my directors to Austin to verify that she was indeed not sick. The next week her entry was still not corrected in the system. When confronted with her misuse of sick leave, she quickly acknowledged her deception and resigned. This did not appear to endear me to her friends or her teacher organization.

I must admit that I did have a little sympathy for her as I had also been replaced in my much younger days for not showing up for work. There will be more on that later.

I guess that might be one of the reasons over the years (in my adult life, that is) I have tried to encourage other folks confronted with circumstances similar to mine to persevere. I liked to use phrases such as "hang in there" or "not to worry" if they felt they were innocent of the allegations against them and, if they were losing their job, told them to accept the situation, build on it, and move on with a new understanding and, hopefully, a new beginning. When dealing with employees, my belief had been that I should always look for a way to have a "good ending." For example, in a previous position at a university, it became necessary to terminate one of my assistants. After some personal counseling, he departed on what I believed to be a "good ending." Approximately a year later, he returned to thank me. He had devoted his previous year to painting, which was his first love. He presented me with two beautiful paintings, which I treasure and still proudly display in my home.

But now the shoe was on my size 13AAA foot. It was now my turn to "hang in there" and "not to worry" and to review the situation and realize this could be a "new beginning" for me.

CHAPTER 4

MY NEW UNDERSTANDING

Micah 6:8 says, "He has shown you, O mortal, what is good. And what does the Lord require of you? To act justly and to love mercy and to walk humbly with your God."

So what created my opportunity for a new beginning? I thought it was just the complaint. Now I am not normally a complainer, but this was not a personal complaint. This complaint was on behalf of the parents of eight students. I had submitted it on an official government form to the appropriate state agency. The teacher had admitted the parents' allegations were true, and they were substantiated by the district's review committee's internal investigation.

I did not have a clue that filing this three-page document would lead to almost three years of turmoil for me and my lovely wife. It seems almost ironic that a three-page, two-paragraph complaint would create so many years of havoc—one year for each paragraph! I wonder what would have happened if it had been a ten-paragraph complaint!

It was also the beginning of a new and very personal understanding of the definition of perseverance. My American Century Dictionary says perseverance is "Continue steadfastly or determinedly; persist."

In addition to a new understanding of perseverance, it was also the beginning of my understanding of the old phrase "The wheels of justice grind slowly." However, because of motions, hearings, and depositions, the next several months were fast-paced, physically tiring, and mentally taxing.

It would have been so much easier to overlook the parents' complaints against the teacher, bow to my boss's demands, and withdraw my whistle-blower complaint. So I continued wondering what in the world possessed me to defy my boss's directive. Why in the world would I not just take the easy way out? I continued to wonder if it was my belief system, some prior experiences, or just my own stubbornness.

Because of my human resources background, my first inclination was to ponder where I might have overlooked something. Had I misinterpreted some policy, rule or regulation, or state statute? Or, indeed, was I just stubborn? Another thought was whether I had placed too much emphasis on what I believed to be my responsibilities in this situation. Did I have some unwritten duty to follow the rules as I understood them? Was I required to file the complaint?

After maturing past my adolescence, I really had tried to follow the rules. Now I must admit that during my adolescence I did not always follow the rules at school. Indeed, occasionally I did get in trouble at school and at home.

However, in this case I firmly believed I had followed the rules in honoring the parents' complaint and filing a whistle-blower complaint. So I wondered how this particular decision could have led to this set of circumstances.

Apparently, I had handled previous issues and complaints pretty well because all of my previous annual evaluations from my previous two superintendents were excellent. In fact the previous school board had appointed me interim superintendent during the search process between the two previous superintendents.

Also in those almost ten years, only a few of my decisions and/or recommendations were questioned requiring some further explanation. But none had ever resulted in a reversal, let alone a personal reprimand, a suspension, or a threat of termination, until now. So I kept asking myself, "Why now? What is behind this continued insistence that I withdraw this official complaint?"

Might it be something seemingly unrelated to me? Just prior to filing the complaint with the SBEC, the school board was embroiled in a continuing internal struggle concerning my previous boss, Superintendent Trujillo. He was hired in 1995, and his contract was extended for five years in 1996. Soon after he was hired, he began a campaign of insisting that any teacher who did not believe that every student could learn should resign. As the old saying goes, you could have heard a pin drop when he made that statement to a district-wide meeting of all eight thousand-plus employees.

Some pushback began when the board wanted to pass a huge capital bond campaign for construction. He opposed it and instead devoted approximately ten million dollars per year out of the annual budget for repairs, renovations, and remodels. When several board members opposed this approach, it appeared to me that he began to ignore them, much to their dismay.

He was a very independent person. I am sure some folks thought he had a very unorthodox management style about him. It was a new experience for me. For example, one midsummer day he came to my office and told me he wanted me to call all eight high school principals and invite them to lunch. As I began to call their offices, I found out that four of them were playing golf at a local country club. He said that was fine and to just tell them to stay there and he would join them for lunch. I called the club and left a message for them to remain there until he arrived. I contacted the other four principals and invited them to join him.

Later that morning, as he was leaving the building, he came by my office and asked me if I wanted to join him because he was going to make a few transfers. Before I got my brain into gear, I said I was just too busy trying to fill all of our vacant teaching positions to go with him. Shortly after he left my office, I suddenly regained my sense of perspective. I realized he was about to create a seismic shift in the assignments of the district's high school principals. So I grabbed my briefcase and rushed out the door to head for the country club to join them.

I wish I could have taken a photo of the faces of the four principals when, as they were leaving the eighteenth hole, they saw us standing in the doorway of the clubhouse. They had not received my message, and they appeared to be very surprised. As we waited for the other four principals to arrive, Trujillo made small talk and told a few jokes, as was his style. I could see the tension growing. After the remaining four arrived, one of the principals finally asked him if this meeting had any specific purpose. That was his opening. He said something like "I am glad you asked," and then one at a time he told them he was reassigning them to a different high school for the coming year. It was easy to see the apprehension grow on their faces as he progressed around the table. As he outlined the school to which each one would be assigned for the coming year, you could see their faces flush.

One principal had only been at her school for a year. When she was the only one left to be reassigned, you could see tears forming in her eyes. You could hear her relief as he told her that, since she had only been there for one year, she would not be moving. The reactions of the other seven were less than enthusiastic.

That afternoon I made the official announcement of the new assignments. Once I made the formal announcement, several board members took immediate umbrage. Apparently, he had not fore-warned them nor asked their permission before making the reas-signments. The board was elected in single-member districts; and each board member wanted to control the personnel working in the schools within his or her district, especially the high schools. Now I was asking myself if this could be a part of my problem because I had made the announcements.

Several board members appeared to remain upset over their loss of control over principal reassignments. So it was not surprising that these actions brought continuing complaints from some members of the board. Several of them told Trujillo he could not make these decisions without their approval. During one board meeting, they contended that they were elected in single-member districts and it was their right to select the principals for the schools in their districts and approve the reassignments of personnel into their districts. He calmly told them to read his contract. That response appeared to me to make some of them furious. I believe this was the night some board members began their yearlong crusade to terminate him.

Looking back, I can see that it might have been one small part of my situation even though it had occurred a couple of years prior to my filing the complaint. It was possible they could have thought I had something to do with the principal reassignments.

These transfers were followed the next year by his making another very controversial decision. In order to budget more funds to the schools, he wanted to reduce the dollars being spent on personnel working in the central office. This meant reducing the number of administrators working there. His plan was to reassign many central office personnel, administrators, and support personnel to vacant positions on one or more of the district's fifty-two campuses. It was my responsibility to sort out how to implement these reassignments. His instructions to me were to follow policy and make sure everyone would be placed in a comparable position at the same salary and that no one would lose his or her job. This move involved shifting approximately fifty individuals. It was accomplished by transferring the current folks to vacant positions on the various campuses and not filling their vacated positions at the central office. The task was formidable and took a couple of months to accomplish. Only one individual refused to be transferred to a new assignment, even though it was at the same salary. Consequently, she eventually lost her job.

Later in my search for reasons I was being directed to withdraw the complaint, I discovered that the one individual who refused a transfer had a personal connection with the board member involved in the complaint.

Because of my position as associate superintendent for human resources, I was administratively tied to the hip of Mr. Trujillo for all personnel decisions. It became clear to me that his decisions were also perceived as mine whether I liked it or not. I must admit that I agreed with most of his decisions because, in my opinion, he always focused on what was good for the students.

The teacher and administrator organizations also expressed their displeasure because, in my opinion, occasionally they had previously been able to lobby the board and impact many personnel decisions including principal and administrator assignments.

The board's displeasure with Trujillo finally erupted into formal charges being filed against him. On October 2, 1998, Ronda Scrivner, president of the board, notified Trujillo of the board's intent to propose his termination. The hearing was held from November 12 through 16, 1998. The board proposed twenty-four allegations in support of his proposed termination. However, the board abandoned thirteen of the twenty-four allegations before the hearing began. I was summoned to testify at the hearing.

During my testimony at his hearing, the board's attorney, Mr. Luther Jones (more on him later), asked me several questions about my knowledge regarding some of the allegations raised against Trujillo. I responded to his questions by stating that I was not aware of all of the allegations he mentioned and that the allegations which had been submitted to human resources regarding the superintendent had been processed according to policy. Mr. Jones appeared to me to be quite flustered at my responses. Apparently, some board members had heard about some allegations and presumed that I had also been informed of them. They must have believed that I had failed to take appropriate action. The insinuation was that I should have convened a review committee to investigate them.

At one point he accused me of not being objective because I was a close friend of the superintendent. He implied that I was too close to him because I seemed to be aware of every other allegation of misconduct within the district. He started asking questions about other complaints which had been filed. These questions were outside of the scope of the Trujillo hearing. He had me under oath and under the authority of the hearing examiner permitting his questioning. I was required to testify at the hearing, or it would be considered insubordination if I did not. To me this was remarkably aggressive and unwarranted questioning by the attorney for the school district.

Regarding questions about other complaints, I responded that other allegations of misuse of students had been officially filed and forwarded to me and they were being handled through the appropriate review process. He then accused me of not following up on the allegations against Mr. Trujillo. Once again, my response was that no allegations had been filed with my office against Mr. Trujillo that had not been properly investigated. This brought a quick retort from him that he did not believe me.

He then wanted to know why a review committee had not been appointed to look at allegations regarding Mr. Trujillo's demanding a principal "hire" his son to be a "volunteer" assistant football coach. I responded that this allegation had been handled in accordance with district policy and the review committee did not find the allegations, as written, to be true. Another item he brought up regarding Mr. Trujillo was why another principal, who supported Mr. Trujillo, was not investigated for using school letterhead paper to request that the parents of his students come forward and support a particular board candidate. My response was that I believed it was investigated by a review committee and the allegations were unfounded. From his questions it was becoming apparent that some board members had a different opinion from mine regarding these issues. It seemed to me that Attorney Jones's areas of inquiry were crafted by the board leadership who had initiated the termination action against their superintendent.

He then asked me questions about my personal relationship with Mr. Trujillo. Specifically, he wanted to know how often we met for lunch and how often I visited him at his home and was I at his home for parties like the one Trujillo recently hosted. He seemed quite surprised when I testified that in all the years that Mr. Trujillo had been my boss, I had been to lunch alone with him only once, the first week of his employment. Also, I had never been to his home; in fact, I did not know where he lived. When I added that he was my boss, not my friend, he dismissed me from the witness stand.

At the conclusion of the hearing, the examiner described the employer–employee relationship between Trujillo and the board thusly:

> he has worked with a School Board that was
> traditionally divided along a 4 to 3 vote line with
> 4 votes being in his favor. In the spring of 1998,

the composition of the 7-person board changed
and the vote became 4 to 3 against. (Opinion of
the hearing examiner; December 9, 1998; page
11; Docket No. 015-LH-1098)

The hearing examiner went on to explain that, shortly after the
election and with this kind of division within the board and a major-
ity of the board members upset with him, his dismissal appeared
to become their obsession. The results of the hearing gave these
four board members grounds to vote to terminate his contract. The
Hearing Examiner's recommendation stated it this way:

"Based on the evidence, the Findings of
Fact and Conclusions of Law, in my capacity as
independent Hearing Examiner, I recommend
the following:

1. In my capacity as Independent Hearing
    Examiner I recommend that Ysleta
    Independent School District proceed with
    the termination of Anthony Trujillo as
    Superintendent.

    SIGNED this the 9th day of December, 1998.
    Juergen Koetter Independent Hearing
    Examiner." (Opinion of hearing exam-
    iner, page 21)

I could not find any reference where the board or their attorney
seemed to mind the inconsistency of charging him with "hiring" his
son as a "volunteer" coach. I must have missed something because
even the hearing examiner included the phrase in his findings.

After some further soul-searching, I began to believe my problems intensified because I had testified in the termination hearing
of Superintendent Trujillo and the implication of my testimony was
supportive of the superintendent. This entire process gave me great

concern. The board created the charges, hired the hearing examiner, used their board's attorney to prosecute the charges, then served as the judges to review the hearing examiner's recommendation and made the final decision.

I am not sure to what Mr. Jones expected me to testify, but my testimony seemed to exacerbate an already difficult relationship between Jones as the board's attorney and me as associate superintendent for human resources. I must admit that I was extremely disappointed with the Hearing Examiner's recommendation and the board's decision because I never personally witnessed any inappropriate actions by Superintendent Trujillo. Also, I supported his focus on the performance of the students in the district.

In the following months it was apparent to me that the board members (President Ronda Scrivner, Charles Peartree, Blanca Dominquez, and Mike Portillo) who voted to terminate Mr. Trujillo's contract were the same individuals who pursued my termination.

After Mr. Trujillo's termination I had the opportunity to review the February 8, 2000 deposition given by Board Member Peartree in my lawsuit. It gave me some valuable insight into his animus toward me when he said:

> Durrett had winked and nodded on some
> complaints and had not filed complaints against
> some others. (Peartree deposition, page 26)

I can only surmise that he was referring to the allegation that Mr. Trujillo demanded a coach "hire" his son as a "volunteer" coach (opinion of the hearing examiner, page 8) because I learned later that the coach making that allegation was a campaign worker for a board member candidate involved with the students. The picture was becoming a little bit clearer for me.

A few days after the board voted to terminate Superintendent Trujillo's contract, they promoted Ms. Irma Trujillo (no relation to Superintendent Trujillo) to be the interim superintendent while the board began a search for a new superintendent.

CHAPTER 5

WAS MY FATE TIED TO MY OLD BOSS?

It was just a couple of months after Mr. Trujillo's termination hearing that the eight sets of upset parents had filed their formal complaint with the human resources division. It was because of their complaint that I felt compelled to file an official complaint with the SBEC. It was clear to me that the parents wanted their children to study for grades and not be bribed. The parents did not approve of their students just walking the streets for approximately two hours and distributing flyers to improve their grades. The fact that they were working for Board President Scrivner and another candidate did not make the project any more acceptable to the parents.

The situation was somewhat convoluted as board member Scrivner had voted to fire Trujillo in 1998 and now the Review Committee was pursuing an investigation concerning allegations which indirectly implicated her. Perhaps my earlier testimony in the Trujillo hearing might have been part of the reason for some of the board members' displeasure with me.

The teacher mentioned in the complaint gave me a little more insight during his deposition, in my lawsuit, on pages 51 and 52. I learned the following:

> Q: Would you agree that the appearance of all of this is that in a school district election involving school board members who can exercise influence over your career, over the career of Mr. B——, that the appearance of this is that you used your position of privilege and influence over students to assist them in their campaign?
>
> A: Assist who?
>
> Q: School board candidates.
>
> A: No. I think this is retaliation, political retaliation on behalf of Mr. Trujillo, because Mr. Trujillo was a witness. He and Mr. Lerma saw me standing in front of Riverside with a picket sign promoting Sandoval's campaign, and they sat there in front of me listening, hearing distance from me. They spent some time there.

It was still not clear to me how I got tied so closely to Mr. Trujillo in decisions and activities of which I was never involved. I got the impression that he believed I filed the complaint because Trujillo was a friend of mine.

Coincidentally, Board President Scrivner and the other candidate involved with the students were the candidates being supported by one of the local teacher organizations in the upcoming election.

While the investigation of this complaint was ongoing, the board hired Dr. Edward Lee Vargas on April 13, 1999, as the new superintendent. He was to assume his duties sometime later. As Dr. Vargas was making his transition from his old position, he made numerous phone calls to me asking for my input—good indications of a productive relationship moving forward I thought. During one phone call, he asked if I had any recommendations. I naively thought this was the beginning of a great working relationship. I responded that, from my perspective as associate superintendent for human resources, I would appreciate it if he would hire another attorney for the district and replace Mr. Jones. When he asked why, I responded that I needed someone who knew more about school law than me or my staff and that Mr. Jones was not up to the task (at the time of my suspension, I wondered if Vargas had ever relayed this conversation to Mr. Jones).

Next, he asked me a very interesting and curious question. He asked me if he could trust me. My response was that he could trust me to always follow state law, the Texas Administrative Code, SBEC rules, and board policies, to the best of my ability. I also told him I would always give him my honest opinion and best advice.

Intermingled with his travels to El Paso, Vargas was being kept up to date on various district activities by Interim Superintendent Irma Trujillo. It didn't take long for Ms. Trujillo to become involved in my complaint which I began to refer to as the "grade inflation issue." It was my opinion that she was being pushed into the process by a couple of school board members, Mrs. Scrivner in particular. It appeared to me that Scrivner wanted to use her position of authority to find out what was happening regarding the investigation because she was one of the individuals potentially involved in the investigation. As a side note it was Scrivner who had recommended Ms. Trujillo to be interim superintendent.

As a part of the investigation, I developed a questionnaire inquiring about board candidates' use of district students in their respective campaigns.

At one point Ms. Trujillo called me into her office and informed me that Dr. Vargas had requested a complete report on the "campaign flyer distribution" allegations involving Board President Scrivner and the other board candidate. It was my personal policy to respond to any board member's question with an executive summary to all board members so that all board members were aware of the inquiry made to me by a board member and all would have the benefit of knowing my response. I prepared a draft of an executive summary for

Interim Superintendent Trujillo on April 29, 1999, to be given to all board members. It outlined the facts which, if true, implicated both the teacher and candidate Scrivner in conduct which possibly violated district policy BBB, Texas Election Code, Code of Ethics, Texas Penal Code, and policy DHA. Item 2.c. of the executive summary contained the following paragraph:

> The students did not indicate that they were given a choice of candidates. Student statements indicate that at least some did not know who they were putting up signs for until they showed up at Riverside High School on Saturday; they were taken to Ronda Scrivner's home where she spoke with them and gave them the campaign materials. The candidates they campaigned for were (candidate X) and Ronda Scrivner.

Later that same day the board's attorney, Mr. Jones, dropped by my office, unannounced, and gave me his unsolicited opinion that the principal had acted inappropriately in reprimanding the teacher involved in the grade inflation incident. He also informed me that the students had constitutional rights and I was wrong in pursuing the allegations. I had to remind him that I was not pursuing the investigation; it was being handled in accordance with board policy. Looking back at that conversation, I now believe he was trying to intimidate me into not following the rules and dropping the investigation without specifically telling me to drop it.

On April 30, 1999, Interim Superintendent Trujillo came to see me. Because I was out of the office, she left a note with my secretary that said, "Dr. Vargas would like for you to get a statement from Ronda Scrivner and (candidate X)."

That was the day after I had prepared the questionnaire for all school board candidates, not just the two he suggested. Later that day I mailed the inquiry to all candidates asking whether or not they had utilized students in their campaigns. Five candidates quickly responded in the negative to my inquiry. Board President Scrivner and the other candidate did not respond.

Immediately after mailing the questionnaire, I began receiving questions from several board members regarding the grade inflation investigation. I had to presume that one faction of the board wanted to discredit Scrivner and the other faction supported her.

In a meeting on May 8, 1999, with Interim Superintendent Irma Trujillo, she said she had talked with Vargas and he wanted a complete review of the grade inflation matter.

On May 12, 1999, I provided Vargas an updated copy of the prior executive summary I had prepared for all board members concerning the investigation's progress. In it I had summarized my complete review of the allegations and information known at that time. I also recommended that statements be taken from additional students. This updated summary now provided additional information, which if true would implicate both the teacher and a board member in conduct which might have violated board policy, the Texas Ethics Code, and Texas law. The salient point of the summary was item 2.d. which stated:

> (The teacher) admitted to (his principal) that he had asked for volunteers and that he promised them 10 points on their mid-term grades. He did not have this activity in his lesson plans nor any curricular rationale or justification. He stated that it was a project. However, he did not seek nor receive any approval for this project. It is still unclear how points will be added to students' grades for an activity not covered by any lesson, assignment, or assessment or whether such can even be done.

On May 14, 1999, over my objection and in violation of district policy, Vargas hired an employee without advertising the position. When I objected, he made it clear to me that he could do what he wanted to do and my objections and board policy didn't matter because he was the superintendent. I continued to insist that we either change the policy or follow it. Maybe that was stupid.

With these developments I now began to seriously question my relationship with Vargas. His disapproval of my desire to follow policy and do what I had promised by following board policy was becoming abundantly clear. Now my new boss and some of the board members appeared to characterize my conduct as obstructive to their aims and agenda.

During the month of May 1999, Vargas began questioning my reports regarding the grade inflation incident. He would press my staff members for information even though he had already received the same information from me. He seemed intent on finding fault with me and/or my staff.

A specific example occurred on June 28, 1999. It involved his contract regarding his life insurance coverage and annuities. His memo stated, in part:

> After repeated requests, the provisions of my contract specifically with regards to life insurance and annuities, your office has still not completed these. Please know that this is unacceptable and I am directing you to move to facilitate the information needed so that this process can be completed. Please provide me with a completion calendar schedule that brings this issue to close no later than Friday, July 9.

When I received the memo directing me to implement the contract language covering his life insurance and annuities, I was somewhat surprised because I had never been given access to his contract. In fact, his contract and all of his other contract-related issues were being handled by the board's attorney, Luther Jones. This issue seemed to disappear when I informed him in response that I did not have access to his contract and that all of his contractual issues were being handled by Mr. Jones.

Originally, I thought it was this kind of personally related issues which led Vargas to look for some issue which he could use to move for my termination. At the same time, I was under the impression that Vargas's supporters on the board were looking for some "dirt" on their colleagues while looking for a way to stop the grade inflation investigation. As time passed and more and more unusual requests and demands for information increased, I was finally getting the picture. Apparently, some board members didn't think I was following the rules. I was a slow learner. My suspicions were later confirmed by Mr. Peartree. In his deposition, in response to the following question from my attorney, he said:

> Q: You think that Dr. Durrett had the right to make a complaint to the SBEC years ago and failed to do so? Is that your belief?
> A: He should have done one on Anthony Trujillo—and never did—if he had been doing his job. (Peartree, page 27)

Following the rules did not seem to be a priority for Vargas. On a couple of occasions, he passed on a request to me from a board member "strongly suggesting" that I hire a particular person. Sometimes it would be for a job opening which had been posted, and sometimes it would be for me to open a position for a particular person. One such example was when he gave me an application and requested that I hire a local judge's wife as a teacher. When I told him I would ask the appropriate HR director to obtain references and then place the application in the appropriate applicant pool, he demanded that I hire her that day. I reminded him that Texas state law concerning "site-based decision-making," board policy, and the Texas State Education Code required that all campus personnel were to be hired by the principal of the campus. It was now quite apparent to me that he was not familiar with Texas education laws, SBEC regulations, the Texas Administrative Code, EEO laws, or board policy.

While Vargas was still transitioning into the district, he continued to make frequent phone calls to district employees. During one of his phone calls to me, he stated that a board member was requesting a detailed update on the grade inflation investigation. So I prepared another executive summary for all board members explaining that the only change was a request by the review committee to obtain additional statements from additional students involved in the distribution of campaign materials. In that summary I also reported that Board Candidates Scrivner and candidate X were the only candidates who had not responded to my questionnaire regarding their use or nonuse of students in the distribution of campaign materials in their respective campaigns.

Consequently, on June 30, 1999, I sent a second request to Board Candidates Scrivner and X asking them to respond to my questions regarding the use of students in their election campaigns. The pertinent paragraph stated:

> On April 30, I forwarded a request for information to you regarding the Ysleta School Board elections. Allegations of unethical conduct have been lodged against a teacher who participated in that day's activities. It is extremely important that I receive all the information which I can gather in order to make a logical and fair recommendation to the Superintendent, concerning these allegations. Therefore, I am attaching a copy of my original letter and requesting that you please respond to the eight questions as soon as possible in order that this investigation may be completed.

Again, they did not respond.

CHAPTER 6

MY OBLIGATION ARRIVES

> Whatever you do, work at it with all your heart, as working for the Lord, not for humans, since you know that you will receive an inheritance from the Lord as a reward. (Colossians 3:22)

When I mailed my complaint on June 30, in accordance with SBEC regulations, I also mailed a certified copy of the SBEC complaint form to Vargas and the teacher. It was interesting to me that both men later denied receiving them (thank goodness for return receipt request forms).

Being the simple-minded administrator that I was, I thought I had done the appropriate thing by reporting an alleged violation of the Administrative Code to the appropriate state agency. I continued to pursue the involvement of the two recalcitrant candidates who had not responded to my questionnaire.

My personal "official" legal troubles and journey through the ole legal process began shortly after mailing that second request to Board President Scrivner and candidate X.

My complaint on behalf of the parents brought a quick response, but to my surprise it did not come from the SBEC. I did not expect the speed or the content of the responses which that complaint generated. The first response was from my boss on Tuesday, July 6, 1999.

This response seemed to come faster than a speeding bullet! I mailed the complaint to the SBEC in Austin, Texas, on June 30. It took him only six days (including the July 4th holiday) to respond. He demanded that I withdraw my complaint. The SBEC had not even had time to review the complaint, so what could possibly have been the motive behind his instant demand that I withdraw it?

My response was that I would review the complete investigative file to make sure I had not missed anything. I continued to evaluate my circumstances and did not respond immediately.

During my previous years with the district, several certified employees had complained to me about unethical conduct of others. However, they had steadfastly refused to file formal complaints alleging code of ethics violations. It was clear that they were afraid of retaliation. This lack of courage had been very frustrating for me because, according to the Texas Administrative Code, I could not file a complaint because I was not a certified teacher in Texas. Being told that ethical violations were occurring and not being able to personally pursue the truth was very disturbing to me.

Just prior to my filing the complaint, the rules changed. Ms. Strashun, SBEC Office of Investigations and Enforcement, confirmed in her written deposition answer to the question:

> No. 6: State whether, as of June 1999, an individual who is not certified by the SBEC under the certification rules of the State Board for Educator Certification had standing to file a complaint with the SBEC relating to the conduct of a certified individual.
>
> Answer: Yes.

Because she answered "yes" to that question, she was then asked to describe the change, to which she responded:

> 19 Texas Administrative Code, Chapter 249, came into law on March 31, 1999. Within that law at Section 249.14, general authority for

filing and processing of non-Code of Ethics complaints is set out. 19 TAC, Section 249.47 (b), pertains to Code of Ethics complaints.

This change was why my frustrations were coming to an end. Now, not only could I file a complaint with the SBEC but I believed I had an obligation to do so.

I remained very confident that it was my obligation to file that complaint. On May 27, 1999, the teacher had given his principal a handwritten note confirming the parents' allegations. His statement included the following:

> Early in April I made a general announcement to all of my classes that I would give extra credit to those students who would volunteer to give up 2 hours of their time on a Saturday morning to community involvement. About 20 students volunteered to meet me at Riverside High School on a Saturday morning at 8:00 AM. After meeting the students at school we all went to a school board Candidate's Head Quarters and helped distribute literature in the neighborhood. For about 2 hours. After 2 hours we left and returned home or to Riverside High School. This is the same information I have shared with you on two different occasions.

Vargas must have really, really wanted me to withdraw it, because three days later, in a meeting on Friday, July 9, he followed his written demand by verbally requesting that I withdraw it. In response to these requests that day, I prepared and mailed a letter to Mr. Cary Decuir, who was the investigator at the SBEC. I stated in part:

> On June 30, 1999, I filed the appropriate complaint forms and the District's investigative file in the (Teacher's) case.

> Dr. Vargas has instructed me to withdraw the complaint and I would appreciate knowing whether or not you have forms for that purpose. If you would please provide me the appropriate information, it would be appreciated.

I also sent a copy of the letter to Vargas.

Later that day, as I said I would, I reviewed the complete investigative file.

On Monday, July 12, 1999, the director of elementary teacher recruitment came to my office and informed me that Dr. Vargas had called him and asked him to accompany me to the superintendent's office. My antennae went up, even though I don't think I am an alien, as this seemed to be an extremely odd request. The only reason I could think of was that Vargas needed a witness for some reason. My boss was very persistent, and I had my suspicions as to why he wanted one of my subordinates as the witness.

During the meeting, it appeared to me that Vargas was very upset and even angry. He had his copy of my July 9, 1999, letter to Mr. Decuir of the SBEC. On the letter he had made five notes he wanted to emphasize. The bottom line was he again demanded that I withdraw the SBEC complaint. He said that the complaint and my motive for filing it were political in nature. Now I was beginning to get a little clearer picture of why he summoned me to a meeting with a witness. Someone did not like me because of his or her perception of my politics. I did not know if it was his perception or a board member's. Then, for the third time, he directed me to withdraw the complaint. I responded that I would reconsider his request and would review the file again.

I did not bother to explain to him that the complaint was not "my" complaint. I was merely the conduit to forward the parents' concerns to the appropriate state agency.

The review committee had recently completed investigating this complaint. I guess I could not let well enough alone, because at the end of the meeting I handed Dr. Vargas the review committee's recommendation regarding their investigation of the teacher. He immediately handed it back to me. He did not sign it or initial it to indicate that he did or did not concur with the committee's recommendation as required by board policy. Then he began a personal verbal assault on me by making critical and demeaning statements to me (poor me).

Later that same day, the employee relations department prepared a decision memorandum, to be forwarded through me to Vargas, in which the review committee recommended the teacher be terminated. I concurred with the recommendation, signed it as associate superintendent, and forwarded it to Vargas. Board policy required that the review committee's recommendation be placed on the school board agenda. Once again Vargas disregarded board policy and did not put it on the agenda. However, he apparently communicated its content to at least one of the board members because the requests for additional information and updates began that day and increased exponentially.

After that meeting, I detected that he began a new tactic. He began putting pressure on me and overtaxing the employees of the HR division with unrealistic demands and deadlines. My workplace quickly became a warzone of flying memos.

The following week, for reasons unknown to me, Vargas requested another copy of the review committee's complete investigative file.

On July 16, 1999, the SBEC responded, through Mr. Decuir, to my inquiry. He stated that a form to withdraw a complaint did not exist.

On August 3, 1999, I made an appointment with Vargas. I personally hand-delivered a cover letter to him informing him once again that the review committee had completed their investigation and attached their decision memorandum. School district policy stated that he or his designee was required to keep the board informed regarding this investigation. The final paragraph of my cover letter stated:

> On July 6, 1999, you directed me to withdraw my complaint. I must respectfully decline.

> I have informed the Office of Investigations and
> Enforcement at the SBEC that my request for a
> form was not a withdrawal of my complaint. I
> would respectively remind you that I have exer-
> cised the rights provided to me by Texas state
> statute and the Texas Administrative Code.

His response was "Well, it looks like we have a problem then."
Wow, my honeymoon with him was much shorter than I had originally believed it would be. He did not like me long before he told
me so. The good news for me was that I no longer had to guess as to
whether or not I had a problem with my boss.

Later that afternoon I went to his office, and I personally
informed Vargas that I had filed a second complaint. This one was
against him, with the SBEC. To my surprise, he seemed surprised.

My cover letter was addressed to Jackie Strashun at the SBEC
and stated in part:

> On July 6, 1999, Ysleta Independent School
> District Superintendent Edward Lee Vargas
> directed me to withdraw a SBEC complaint
> which I had filed earlier regarding (the teacher).
> I believe that Edward Lee Vargas has intention-
> ally attempted to deny me or impede me in the
> exercise of a professional right or privilege to file
> a complaint with the State Board for Educator
> Certification, in accordance with State Law and
> the rules of the Texas Administrative Code.

By now my naivety had disappeared, and my confidence in
the "system" had evaporated. I asked my coordinator of employee
relations to prepare copies of my complaint for mailing to the SBEC
and address the return receipt for certified mail forms. I also asked
him if he had any advice for me. His instant response was "You better hire a lawyer." I don't think he was surprised when I responded

that I had already retained a lawyer. Thankfully, as it later turned out, he did mail them certified and requested a return receipt for both letters.

Vargas, in a meeting on August 4, repeated his dissatisfaction with what I had done. It was a heated discussion, and from that moment on I was positive about what was happening. It was also clear that one or more board members were actively pushing Vargas to find a way to force me to withdraw my SBEC complaint. It was also clear that my termination was high on somebody's list.

On August 5 I received a memo from him which stated, in part:

> Please notify me by noon tomorrow the statutes and Texas Administrative Code provisions which you reference in your memorandum of August third in support of your decision to deny my administrative directive that you withdraw a complaint filed by you against (the teacher) with the State Board for Educator Certification.

As I stated earlier, he was not familiar with the education laws and the education codes of Texas and, apparently, was not in a hurry to get familiar.

Late that evening I provided his office with forty-five pages of documents containing all pertinent statutes and a copy of the Texas Administrative Code provisions which I had referenced in my August 3 memo and which I had used as the basis for my authority to file my complaints.

Next, on August 9 I filed an internal grievance against Vargas utilizing the district's grievance policy. My grievance alleged that he had subjected me to retaliation for filing a lawful complaint with the SBEC. I sent him a copy of my grievance and a memo explaining the grievance policy as outlined in board policies.

Now the tag team of emails was on! On that same day I received his response. The reference line simply said, "Administrative Directive." This delivery was the formal beginning of a two-plus-year ordeal that changed my life forever. His memo was short and to the point. It read:

> In your August 3, 1999, memo you indicated that you were declining my directive to you from July 6, 1999 to withdraw your formal complaint to the State Board for Educators Certification regarding (the teacher). I would like you to reconsider your decision and advise me before the end of the day. Thank you. (Signed: Dr. Edward Lee Vargas, Superintendent)

Now everything was really speeding up. Once again Vargas seemed to be growing impatient and wanting quick answers as he gave me "lots of time," as the end of the day, to reconsider my decision. I guess he thought I was not serious when I filed my complaint. In my opinion he still thought he could intimidate me into withdrawing it.

Before the end of that day, I dutifully responded as he requested. My answer was also short and to the point. I responded:

> I just received your August 9, 1999, request asking me to reconsider my prior decision not to withdraw my formal complaint against (the teacher). When you first requested that I review the file, I did that, and again concluded that my decision was based upon good and substantial evidence to let my complaint stand. I in no way wish to be insubordinate but I must respectfully decline your directive to withdraw my complaint.

I am pretty sure that he did not care whether or not I did not wish to be insubordinate. He must have worked overtime that night to get me out of the way as soon as possible.

When I arrived at work on August 10, a district security guard was waiting for me in front of my office door. Now I would not say the guard was lurking in the hall, but he was "Johnny on the spot" when I approached my office door. He ushered me into my office and directed me to "remove all of my personal items from my desk." He then asked me to leave the building.

Later that evening, while at home, a district security guard delivered me the following notice:

> Effective immediately, you are suspended with pay, pending a determination by the Board of Trustees of whether or not you should be given notice of termination for cause for violation of one or more provisions of the District's Policies and Procedures, among which I will propose for inclusion violation of district policy DFBA-R, 4. Should the Board of Trustees decide to issue a notice of proposed termination, you shall have the right to appeal their decision to the State Commissioner of Education who will in turn appoint a hearing examiner to take sworn testimony on issues related to your employment status. Upon completion of the hearing process, the hearing examiner will issue findings of fact and conclusion of law, to be thereafter acted upon by the Board of Trustees.

I did not need to read any further than the first line of the letter to know my life was about to undergo a drastic change. It no longer mattered whether or not I would withdraw the complaint. I was about to embark on a new challenge, and there was no turning back.

The notice did include the information that I had a right to appeal. *Big deal*, I thought. A right to appeal—that only meant more attorney's fees and more delays at the state level. This was also a nice try at attempting to derail my legal rights. If I followed this advice, I would foreclose my appeal because, according to SBEC policy, first I was required to exhaust all administrative remedies required by the district.

I already knew that it would be one avenue I could use to appeal my termination if the local board sided with Vargas. But an appeal to the Commissioner of Education would be a long shot.

Now I began to wonder. What in the world would possess me, a man in his right mind, I thought, to be so stubborn? What in my past would train, instruct, guide, or encourage me to refuse a direct order from my boss knowing I probably would be fired if I refused? Was my sense of duty to follow the rules pounded into me at an early age? *How in the world did I get to this point?* What made me so convinced that I was right? What was right? What did influence me? Why would I do this at this point in my career? I had responsibilities to my family, and I was not ready for a long-term layoff, job search, or retirement.

What, if any, were my "seemingly unimportant moments"? Why didn't I just withdraw the complaint, walk away, and get on with life? What formed my character? What possessed me to ignore the fact that the president of the school board might be implicated in the complaint? Any smart fellow (by now you know that did not apply to me) would know that it was going to cause some very personal problems. Well, maybe, just maybe, I wasn't very smart. I am sure some folks would agree.

7

Did My Younger Days Influence Me?

Now that I was suspended, I had time to reflect on what was happening and question why I was entangled in this legal struggle. There were lots of memories of the twists and turns during my growing-up years that helped me understand why I had not withdrawn my complaint. I had time to think about what influenced me in the development of my character, whatever it was. I had learned at an early age to work hard. This is another part of the legacy that my dad left me. He pounded into us kids that hard work, honesty, and the need for a good education were the keys to success. However, just because he left it for me didn't mean I picked it up right away!

As a teenager I had what I considered a great job. It was one at which I eventually got an early lesson on following the rules. I got to ride my bicycle all over town and get paid. Who could ask for anything more? Every Saturday I would ride the two miles to the Western Union office and report in by 8:00 a.m. Mrs. Ribble (a wonderful lady) expected me to follow her rules and be ready to begin work at exactly eight o'clock. That meant I had to arrive early and have the mop bucket filled with warm soapy water, the can of Bon Ami in hand, and a squeegee and a clean rag ready by eight. The first order of the day was to wet the rag and wash the front windows with Bon Ami, use a squeegee to remove the water, and then dry the windows with a clean rag. Once the windows were clean, the next chore was to sweep the office floors as she was receiving the morning telegrams on the Telex machine. Once she cleared the Telex machine and prepared the telegrams for delivery, she would arrange them by location in town; and then I was off zooming around town on my bicycle delivering them. What a wonderful time it was for me, riding my bike and making money. *Wow*! That was living.

During this same time frame, after football practice or basketball practice, I also teamed up with my good buddy Jere Beasley to deliver pianos for Bingham's Music Store. This job eventually created a dilemma for me. Delivering pianos paid a lot more than delivering telegrams. So I spent Christmas Eve delivering pianos and did not report to work to deliver telegrams. Now I knew I should have at least called the office. I did not follow the rules. I did not contact Mrs. Ribble to tell her I would not be coming to work. So I was not surprised the following Saturday when I went to the Western Union office and my friend Billy Bob (now that seemed fitting; at least he had Bob in his name) had replaced me. *Lesson learned*: Follow the rules! Why? Because sometimes a short-term gain could lead to a long-term loss. But I was lucky; in this situation I still made more money delivering pianos than I had made delivering telegrams. But I did lose that additional cash from Western Union.

While I was in junior high, we moved to a house on the Lovington highway which was a couple of miles from the junior high and high schools. With the exception of when we were living on the farm, every place we lived we had to walk to school because we were not in the "bus zone." But we didn't care because we didn't mind walking. Occasionally, I got a treat when one of my older brothers' friends would drop by and give him a ride to school; and they would let me ride with them.

The Wise family lived directly across the highway from us. They had a small farm outside of town on the Bethel highway. Most weekends and holidays Ken and Neal Wise were responsible for going to the farm and feeding the cows. I loved to go with them because we could "horse" around. By horsing around I mean we could ride the cows and have a great time. On Christmas Eve of 1950, Ken and Neal asked me if I wanted to go with them.

My goodness, I could not resist. A game we played as we drove to their farm was to guess what car model was approaching. The first to guess the model of the car won a point. On this Christmas Eve, we were busy concentrating on the upcoming traffic. I was riding in the rear seat on the passenger side of a 1947 Plymouth. For those of you who don't remember that model, the rear doors opened "backward." If you opened the door while the car was moving, it caught the wind.

As we bumped along the Bethel highway, my door began to rattle; and the wind made a lot of noise, so I wanted to close it. An eleven-year old boy, in heated competition of guessing what the next car model would be, worried about the noise the car door was making. Well, I pushed down on the handle of the door holding it tight, and the wind caught the door and yanked me to the edge of the running board. This little trip gave me a new meaning for "gone with the wind."

I will never forget being yanked to the edge of the running board, falling forward, and looking down at the pavement as it rushed past. It is still hard for me, even today, to believe what I remember about that ordeal. My mind was processing what was going to happen as my body was being gradually extracted from the car. I say gradually because it seemed like I was being pulled out in slow motion. I could see the pavement and gravel bar ditch rushing past. My brain was telling me that if I just let the door pull me out of the car, I would fall forward, the door would catch my legs and swing my body around, and my head would fall under the rear tires. So I jumped. As I flew through the air into the bar ditch, I could see myself just missing the rural mailboxes lined up along the highway. When the Wise boys recounted the event, they said it was a miracle that I had missed the mailboxes. No one could tell me how far I rolled or slid along that bar ditch. I did not remember landing! I guess that was one reason they referred to those car doors as suicide doors. So my questions to myself were and are: Why in the world didn't I just pull myself back into the car? How did I survive? Only God knows.

My last memory of that Christmas Eve is waking up in Doctor Thetford's office. My mom and the doctor kept telling me to be still as they continued removing small bits of gravel from my face, arms, and legs. My body was raw from head to toe as the gravel had acted like sandpaper and scraped most of the skin off of my arms and legs as I rolled and tumbled over the gravel. Thank goodness for a shirt and pants. The nurse spent a very long time digging the gravel out of my skin as my mom watched and cried. It was weeks before I could walk or move my arms without cracking a scab open and start bleeding. It was a miracle to me and my family that I survived that little jump. An even bigger miracle was that I did not have any broken bones because I was told we were traveling between sixty and seventy miles per hour when I jumped.

In 1955 we moved from our house on the Lovington Highway to a home on South Avenue D. I refer from house to home because this was the first time we were not share croppers or renters. It was the first home Mom and Dad ever owned—they and the bank, of course. This was where I met one of my lifelong friends, Jere Beasley. He lived across the street with his grandmother, Granny Ryan. We spent many days roaming the town together on our bicycles.

CHAPTER 8

THAT EARLY EDUCATION THING
(OR MY MISGUIDED EDUCATIONAL PURSUITS)

In junior high I managed to make the honor roll and was exempt from my ninth grade final exams. I was so proud of myself! But I could not let well enough alone; and once again my tongue overrode my brain, like a flood over a cliff. True to form, I could not keep my mouth shut because the lesson I learned in the first grade had long been forgotten.

During the time for the final exam for biology, I was on the football field with a lot of my friends when a student assistant summoned me to return to biology class. My teacher said I had not turned in my class project, so I was not exempt and must take the final exam. Well, I just could not let this stand, so I hurried up the stairs to her classroom. As soon as I entered the room, I shouted at her telling her she did not know what she was talking about. I was exempt from her test. I began shuffling through the papers on her desk looking for my project paperwork. She broke down in tears. Her student assistant rushed out of the room and down the stairs to the principal's office. Before I could get through the papers on her desk, Mr. Livingston, the principal, burst into the room shoving students and empty chairs out of his way. He grabbed me by my collar and whisked me down to his office. He plopped me into a chair with the admonition that I stay put as he left the office.

Unlike my earlier experience with Ms. Lillian, when she put tape over my mouth and broke rulers over my hands, these consequences were going to be quite different.

When he finally returned, he handed me a note addressed to my parents. He then informed me I should get out of his office, out of the building, and off school property. I was not to return until I returned with both of my parents. Boy, oh boy, I was in trouble now! I was not only in trouble at school; but, Lord oh mercy, my dad was going to give me a "licking" for not following the rules. What could I possibly say? All of my troubles were of my own making.

Mr. Livingston's note to my folks explained my actions and that I was suspended from all school activities. The note also emphasized that I would not be promoted to the tenth grade unless and until both of my parents accompanied me to his office. My dad was an extremely hardworking fellow. He worked on road jobs, and he rarely worked in Portales or even close enough to come to school during the workweek without missing a day of work (without pay I might add). My goodness, he was mad and rightfully so. Now he was the disciplinarian of our home. If Mother thought one of us youngsters deserved to be disciplined, we could not leave the house on Friday nights until Dad got home. He would administer his form of discipline, usually with a razor strap.

When I finally made it to school with my parents, they were in for another big surprise. As it turned out, so was I. Apparently Mr. Livingston believed he should help me clean the slate with my parents. Dad learned that I was not only in trouble for my actions with Ms. Cooper but also for some of my earlier escapades during the year. He related to them that on one other notable event I had helped stage a school walkout. I was one of the "beagle boys" creating a protest about something. To this day I still do not remember what it was about. I do remember the beagle boys making some chocolate chip cookies for a joke. We used those little ex-lax squares for the chocolate chips. Mr. Livingston was not pleased with that either. When he told my folks that I had taken a rattlesnake out of its glass container, tied a string around it, and lowered it from the second floor classroom window, I thought my mom was going to faint. I did not have the heart to tell them that I was there, but I did not have the courage to touch it. My dad was not proud of me that day, and I could tell because I got a real blistering when I got home for not following the rules.

After I apologized to the world for everything I had been caught doing or had been accused of doing, things settled down for the summer, and I was eventually promoted to high school.

CHAPTER 9

THOSE HIGH SCHOOL DAYS

To my surprise my first experience as a sophomore in high school was not a pleasant one. My first class of my first day in high school was geometry. The teacher's "role-taking" process that first day was to pass a sheet of paper up and down each isle for each one of the students to sign his or her name on it. When the paper was returned to her desk, she began looking directly at each of us as she read each name. When she came to my name, she almost shouted, "Bob Durrett, if you are any kin to Jerry Durrett, you get up and get out of here right now."

I believe that is an exact quote. Needless to say, it was not a flattering way to enter high school; but it sure was memorable. At least I will never forget it. My classmates harassed me about that for years. As it turned out, my brother Jerry was a much better math student than I was; and I bet before the year was over she was wishing Jerry was back in her class instead of me.

My visitations to the principal's office did take a break for a while, for my entire sophomore year as I recall.

As a junior in high school, my chemistry class became very informative for me. It was here that hydrogen sulfide became a reality known to me not just as a formula but as "rotten egg gas." Whew, does that stuff stink! Our teacher was a very bright old maid who had worked on the Oak Ridge, Tennessee, nuclear projects during WWII. When she became focused on putting formulas or drawing diagrams on the blackboard, she was in her own world. While she was at the blackboard, she was oblivious to what was occurring in the classroom behind her back. For example, during experiments requiring heat, we would remove the Bunsen burners from under the beakers to disrupt her experiments. Once she remarked that she could not understand why some of her simple experiments did not work. Shooting "water spurts" at classmates from the water outlets in the sinks was a favorite activity until some "spurts" hit the chalkboard. Now that got her attention.

What in the world would she have thought if she knew that we were planning to use what she had taught us in some nefarious manner? Some of my buddies and I planned to release rotten egg gas on the visiting choral groups who were coming for district competition. Well, they came, and we released several quart jars of that smelly aroma on one of the choirs during their performance. Apparently, we were not very subtle because I landed in the principal's office one more time. He gave me and my cohorts the chance to improve our penmanship by informing us that each of us had to write an apology letter to every one of the visiting choirs. Writing letters would not have been too bad except that he had to proofread and approve every letter before we could mail them. It took several rewrites for me as my "writing skills" were not as proficient as my tongue.

During high school my study habits became less than important to me except in order to play sports. All athletes had to maintain a C grade average to participate in athletics. Football and basketball were a passion for me, so I made sure I maintained a C average so I could be on the team traveling squad.

Financially, my family was not "in the money," so to speak. We did not take vacations like many of the other students. Before making the football traveling squad, I had never spent a night in a motel. I can only remember two out-of-town "attempted" vacations with the family. I use the term "attempted" because one ended almost before it began when the old car broke down within sixty miles from home outside of Tatum, New Mexico. The other attempt was a family reunion when we all camped out in Zion National Park. Therefore, being on the traveling squad was extremely important to me. I was motivated.

I loved the fact that, if you were on the football or basketball traveling squads, you got to make trips to other towns and sometimes sleep in a motel. Wow! What a thrill for me! I will always remember a trip the junior varsity basketball team made to a basketball tournament in Hobbs, New Mexico. After we lost the first game on Thursday night, we were scheduled to play a team from Texas the next morning. When we got up the next morning, the coaches had us check out of the motel. Now, if we won on Friday, we would get to stay another night and play again on Saturday.

By checking out of the motel, I guess the coaches did not think we would win the next game. They were almost right. We could not make a basket during the first half. By halftime we were down by over twenty points. During halftime Coach Fitt was encouraging. He told us we were hustling and trying and we should not give up and just keep hustling. He said we should begin the second half with a half-court press. My only claim to basketball fame came during that halftime when I asked the coach if we could press full-court instead. He said, "Go for it"; and we did. We won that game and checked back into the motel. Boy, was I proud and happy!

Later that evening we saw one of the coaches get into a taxi and return sometime later with a brown paper bag in his hand. We wondered.

Ah, a new opportunity for the curious. As the noise level increased in the coaches' room, we wondered what in the world they were talking so loudly about. The cinder block walls carried the noise, but we could not make out what they were saying. Now we just had to know, right? Well, the only thing to do was to remove the cover on the electrical outlet between our rooms so we could hear what was being said. Needless to say, none of us were electricians; but we thought we had to find a way to hear what was being said. Just after we removed the electrical outlet cover on the wall between our room and the coaches' room, the fingernail file we were using as a screwdriver touched the wrong wires and sparked; and, poof, the lights in the motel went out. Cockroaches could not have disappeared any faster than we did. You have never seen teenage boys scramble so fast to get into bed.

My traveling squad experiences ended with basketball season my senior year. I wanted to try out for the baseball team. If I made the traveling squad I might have gotten another night in a motel. That was the year of my first attempt at playing baseball in high school. It was a very short-lived experience. The ball diamond was about a mile or so from the high school, so Coach Batson had the team run from school to the ballpark. Unlike some of the team, I did not smoke. However, I had seen the pros chewing tobacco; so that had to be my vice of choice. On the first day of tryouts, I was sitting on the fender of the equipment pickup talking with a buddy as we waited on the coach to arrive. I had a big wad of Beech-Nut tobacco in my mouth, chewing and spitting like I was somebody. The coach walked up beside me; and when I started to jump down, he gently grabbed my arm and said something like "No need to get down. You have not followed the rules. You will not be playing this season." So that ended my long and lustrous baseball career without even setting foot on the diamond—something about following the rules.

Playing football and basketball during junior high and high school was one of my real pleasures. I was lucky enough to get to play in almost every football game either on the junior varsity or varsity team and never have an injury. However, when I say "playing basketball" in high school, that is a little deceiving. In actuality, I mostly warmed the bench. But, occasionally, I did get to play a little. It was during one of those "little playing times" that I received a small cut above my right eye during a game in Roswell, New Mexico. I was bleeding like I was really injured, but I was not feeling a thing when Coach Smith came bursting onto the court yelling at the referees to stop the game so he could stop the bleeding.

With that one exception, my athletic career had been basically injury-free until the end of my junior year. Then I tried out for the track team. Ye old high school was not blessed with the state-of-the-art equipment. For a chin-up bar we were using a pipe stuck between two tree branches. The pipe was bent in the middle and would swivel from time to time during exercises; so we, of course, were not supposed to be using it. One warm and breezy afternoon, I was attempting my "pullovers," that is, swinging my legs up and over the bar attempting to move into a pushup position above the bar. As the bar twisted, I lost my balance, falling facedown onto the pipe. When I finally woke up, I was in the doctor's office (seems like I have been in this predicament before). This time I was with Dr. Loree and his nurse, Coach Smith's wife; they were working on me. They explained that, when I hit the bar, it pushed my two front teeth into my nasal cavity. It took a considerable amount of time for them to extract most of the shattered pieces of bone fragments. As a matter of fact, small pieces of bone shards continued to work their way out of my gums for many, many years. My face was so swollen after the accident that I was barely recognizable for several weeks.

Apparently, my citizenship improved during my senior year in high school because I was discipline-free. The best example of my good citizenship was a trip to the state student council's convention. I was able to convince our principal, Mr. Shields, that I should be allowed to attend the student council convention which was to be held in Raton, New Mexico, during December. Most of my class-mates who attended the convention were surprised that I was allowed to attend because I had never been elected to any student govern-ment office. I, of course, attributed my attendance to my powerful and eloquent appeal to Principal Shields. I explained to him that I should be allowed to attend specifically because I had never been elected to a student government office and that I needed to learn more about it. For once my big mouth paid off!

This proved to be a very interesting trip. You see, Raton, New Mexico, is just across the Raton Pass from Trinidad, Colorado, where they sold 3.2 beer to anyone eighteen years old. I just happened to be eighteen at the time (remember I had two tries at the first grade), and some in the group wanted some beer. Well, the challenge was on! How to get to Trinidad? One of our sponsors drove us to Raton in a blue, four-door Studebaker station wagon. After a short discussion, I convinced some of the group that it would be a simple matter to use the tinfoil off of a gum wrapper to hotwire the car. So, during one workshop session, I hotwired the car; and off we went over Raton Pass. The eighteen miles over the pass was uneventful until we started down into Trinidad. Snow was beginning to fall, so we felt we needed to hurry. Once the purchase was made, we hurriedly headed back as the snowfall became very heavy. The trip then became a little more exciting when the tinfoil wrapper dropped off the ignition switch and the car came to a quick halt. Frantically, we were grabbing at the tinfoil and trying to reinsert it into position. After what seemed like a very long time, we got the tinfoil back in place, restarted the car, and headed for the motel. When we arrived in the parking lot, it was now full; and the previous location of the car was occupied. Oh, no! Now where to park? That was the first question. We had taken the car from a parking space close to the entrance, and now we had to park it in the back of the parking lot. What would our sponsor think when she came back to the car? This was a second question which I never heard answered. She was a wonderful, kind, smart lady; so I am sure she figured it out that the car had been moved, but probably not the beer trip thing. I don't believe the principal ever found out about this little escapade.

CHAPTER 10

FOLLOWING POLICY

On August 12, 1999, in accordance with district policy, I filed a second grievance against Vargas for violating the Texas Whistle-Blower Act (TWBA) by suspending me. In that complaint I was seeking, among other things, full reinstatement of my employment with the district.

This grievance recited the basic essentials of a whistle-blower complaint and recited the relevant portions of district policies governing TWBA complaints. It is interesting to note that the signs which the human resources division posted prominently in every building of the district stated in bold letters:

> Retaliation Prohibited by State Law. A state or local governmental body may not suspend or terminate the employee of, or otherwise discriminate against, a public employee who reports a violation if the employee report is made *in good faith*. (Vargas, Exhibit 39) (Emphasis added)

I guess he must have thought that I did not file my complaint in good faith, but he never asserted it in any of his allegations.

Almost before the ink was dry on my suspension letter, Vargas met with the staff of the human resources division *on August 12, 1999*. He told them that I would not be returning. I thought this was a little presumptuous since neither of my two local grievances had been heard and the SBEC had not taken any action on my whistle-blower complaint and the board had not voted to fire me, "yet." He then introduced my replacement as the interim executive director for human resources. Later a couple of "my old staff" called me and said they were a little puzzled because the position Vargas identified as being held by my replacement did not exist in the budget and had not been advertised as required by the district's EEO policy. Apparently, once again, this did not concern either Vargas or the board because no action was taken to enforce board policy and nullify this hiring.

The following day, August 13, at a meeting of all principals in the district, Vargas doubled down and announced that "Durrett would not be back." I must admit, when I was informed about this announcement, I still believed and hoped that he was just a little premature in announcing my permanent departure.

It was really interesting to me that the position of interim executive director for human resources was not in the budget. Just the night before the board had added an action item to a *supplemental agenda* regarding the need to reduce budgets. Agenda item 323 stated:

> Take up and consider whether or not a determination should be made that a financial exigency and/or a need for one or more program changes exists in sufficient magnitude to justify remedial action by the Superintendent.

When I called the HR office inquiring about the "interim executive director for human resources job," I was informed that on August 4 my replacement had taken an application to HR. When he was asked for which position he was applying, he responded that he did not know but that Vargas had told him to take his application to them. From the date of my replacement's application, it appeared that Vargas was confident on August 3 that my suspension and termination was not only imminent but permanent.

Now that the district had hired an interim executive director for human resources, I believed that he would be assigned as hearing officer for my grievances against Vargas. And, sure enough, Vargas appointed him to hear my appeal (Vargas deposition, page 213). Then I knew I was in trouble because it was my firm belief, regardless of his ethics, that he was not going to rule against his new boss who had just recruited him.

On August 18, 1999, Vargas personally corresponded with Jackie Strashun at the SBEC. He sent the following letter to her:

> I recently received a copy of Robert Durrett's letter to you dated August 3, 1999 (copy attached). His self-serving interpretation of my conduct—never shared with me—is unworthy of a response.
>
> I did request Dr. Durrett to withdraw his complaint pending review by my office and/or the Board of Trustees. An investigation is currently underway into Durrett's real motives for his ex parte pursuit of a complaint against (the teacher). Until these matters are resolved, I respectively request that the complaint be withdrawn and any further action by your agency be suspended.
>
> If additional information is necessary, please do not hesitate to contact me. I will await your acknowledgement of this request.

At 6:00 p.m. that afternoon, I received a hand-delivered letter notifying me that a level 2 grievance conference had been scheduled for Monday, August 23, at 9:00 a.m. in the board conference room. When the conference began, my first question to him was "If you find in my favor on either of these two grievances, do you have the authority to overrule the prior decisions made by Dr. Vargas?"

He appeared to be a little taken back. His response was "You have only filed one grievance."

When I told him he needed to review the files because I had filed two separate grievances, he responded that he would. Then when I asked him again if he had been given the authority to overrule Vargas, he stated that he would "try to influence Vargas." In other words, in my opinion, he had not considered that possibility.

During the grievance conference, Lawyer Jones asked me some unrelated questions regarding other allegations about which he had heard. I responded that the meeting was to discuss my grievances and only the allegations upon which my grievances were based. When I explained that the allegations he mentioned had not been filed, his response was inexplicable to me. He once again accused me of being on a political witch hunt against a board member. It was surprising, because neither of my two grievances had anything to do with a board member. I wondered what was he worried about.

It goes without saying that I was not surprised when my grievances for adverse employment actions were dismissed and my requested remedies were denied. But I still had an appeal left, as slim as it was, to the school board. However, my hope of a successful appeal was like hoping that I would eventually have plastic surgery and look like Robert Redford.

On September 6, 1999, SBEC supervising attorney in the investigations and enforcement division, Jacqueline Strashun, had prepared a *legal analysis of ethics complaints* document. She submitted her recommendation through her immediate supervisor, Ron Keller, to Pamela Tackett, executive director, regarding the (teacher) matter. Her recommendation stated in part:

> The complaint should be approved in its entirety. It contains sufficient facts to support the alleged violations of the Educators' Code of Ethics.

It appeared that some positive things were beginning to happen at the SBEC regarding my complaint. I put on my happy camper smile.

Apparently, the board was not aware of the SBEC recommendation or didn't care because, two days later on September 8, 1999, the board voted to:

> ...approve that notice of proposed termination be sent out to the employee in question as discussed in closed session, seconded by Mr. Peartree.

> Aye: Mrs. Scrivner, Ms. Dominguez, Mr. Peartree, Mr. Portillo, and Ms. Sada
> No: Mr. Sanchez and Mr. Legarreta

I attended that meeting to see about whom they were talking because the name of that proposed individual was not listed on the posted agenda. Even though my name was not mentioned, I was pretty sure they were referring to me. And, before the vote was taken, I was pretty sure that the unnamed person was "little ole me." How did I know? In reviewing the personnel section of the agenda, item 7 came before item 11; and the motion to terminate someone was item 7. So I was positive when the motion was made under item 11, administrative personnel, to:

> ...approve the Interim Executive Director for Human Resources made by Mrs. Scrivner, seconded by Ms. Sada... Motion passed. (Board minutes)

I knew this person was about to replace me even though no decisions had been rendered regarding my two grievances or my SBEC complaint. My understanding of the situation was what has frequently been referred to as seeing "the writing on the wall."

I also knew I was destined to meet the board again as soon as they realized they had made the mistake of not posting my name on the agenda. That fact kept my comfort level pretty high because I knew I would be receiving that old paycheck for a few more months.

To this day I still believe that the board's purpose was to derail the review committee's grade inflation investigation because it could possibly involve Board President Scrivner. By terminating my employment, I believe that some of the board members must have believed they would also stop the SBEC investigation. "Why?" some folks might ask. My belief is that by terminating me it would intimidate other employees. What employee in his or her right mind was going to pursue this particular investigation, or any investigation, when they knew I was fired for exercising a lawful fundamental right and bringing an issue to the attention of the public?

I believe that getting fired for filing a whistle-blower complaint is a major reason folks do not file whistle-blower complaints. I believe it because I hear about whistle-blowers being fired, but I am not aware of any whistle-blower being supported by a state agency or federal agency.

After the meeting adjourned, I asked the board's lawyer, Mr. Jones, whom the board had voted to propose to terminate. With a straight face, he said, "You (meaning me, ole big-eared Bob)." Remember this was the lawyer whom I had requested that Vargas replace because I believed I knew more education law than he did. Also, my coordinator of employee relations absolutely knew more school law than me and Jones combined. Anyway, I informed Jones that it was impossible for the board to fire me that night because state law required that, in order to fire me, my name must be listed on the agenda (not because of who I was but because of my position as associate superintendent). The purpose for this regulation is to inform the public of impending action against a senior administrator. This notice allows the public to speak for or against the proposed action.

Because my name was not listed on the agenda, it would have been impossible for anyone to speak on my behalf. In my situation it was just in case some poor misguided soul might have wanted to stick his or her neck out and speak on my behalf. I told the lawyer I would sue him personally if my paychecks stopped.

Apparently, my little threat did not bother Mr. Jones because the next day I received my first notice of proposed termination from the president of the Board of Trustees. The first paragraph stated:

> In accordance with Ysleta Independent School District policy and procedure, you are hereby notified that the Board of Trustees proposes to terminate your contract of employment.

The letter was hand-delivered to my home the next evening, September 9, 1999. It contained four charges which the board believed to be terminable offenses I had committed. They were:

1. On or about June 30, 1999, without authority of the Superintendent, nor notification to the Board of Trustees, you filed a complaint with the State Board for Educator Certification seeking a revocation of the teaching credentials of a district faculty member (teacher).

2. On or about July 6, 1999, Superintendent Edward Lee Vargas directed you to withdraw the complaint against (teacher).

3. On or about August 3, 1999, you failed to comply with Superintendent Vargas's directive and initiated severe disciplinary action against (teacher) without the knowledge or consent of either Superintendent Vargas or the Board of Trustees.

4. On or about August 5, 1999, you failed to provide Superintendent Vargas documents which purport to justify your refusal to withdraw the complaint.

In the final sentence I was referred to my replacement, the new executive director for human resources, if I had any questions. The letter was signed "Sincerely" by the board president. Now that was sweet, a sincere proposed notice of termination.

It was now crystal-clear to me that my options were severely limited. Believing that I could not win by playing on their court and by their rules, I contacted my lawyer and reported what had transpired. He began preparations for filing a lawsuit.

Also on September 9 SBEC Executive Director Pamela Tackett had approved Jackie Strashun's September 6 recommendation to approve my code of ethics complaint regarding (the teacher). It now appeared that a hearing would finally be forthcoming. I was feeling very confident that the SBEC was going to take some action, mistakenly confident as it turned out.

On September 13, 1999, I filed yet another internal grievance challenging the improper posting of my position for termination and challenging the board's improper consideration of my termination. It is interesting to note that this improper posting was initiated by Board President Scrivner (yep, the same lady implicated in the grade inflation complaint) and Vargas. This grievance also directly challenged my suspension and the board's improper notice of proposed termination under the Texas Whistle-Blower Act.

By filing my September 13 grievance, I believed I was fulfilling my legal obligation to exhaust all administrative procedures. Feeling very confident of my actions, I believed it was now time to get really serious and go on the offense.

The board's legal maneuvering over the next two-plus years gives you a clue as to the length to which some politicians will go, with taxpayers' money of course, to protect their own skin. Motions and counter-motions were about to begin. I was continually amazed that the SBEC complaint was so short and the legal maneuvering in trying to justify my proposed termination was so long, expensive, and involved.

On September 16 I notified SBEC's Strashun of my suspension and requested that all further correspondence to me be sent to my home address. I guess my suspension was a nonevent to them or their interoffice communication was a little slow because she mailed her next letter addressed to me at the school district. Go figure.

If you believe, as I had believed, that whistle-blowers are protected and supported by some governmental agency, you are wrong! Why did I believe that you might ask. Well, now the good old boy network sprang into action. On September 17 I received a weird letter from SBEC's Pamela Tackett, executive director (Strashun's supervisor), requesting more information with regard to the (teacher) complaint. At first it was confusing because on September 10 she had already accepted my complaint for prosecution. I later responded and notified her that I had been suspended and did not have access to district files.

Now I have never worked in a fish market, but I thought I could smell something fishy. Why? That same day, the seventeenth, SBEC Attorney Jacqueline Strashun wrote (the teacher) offering him some settlement opportunities. It now appeared that someone at the SBEC was bowing to pressure. I just did not know for sure from where the pressure was coming. Was it within the agency? If it came from within, just how far up the SBEC chain of command was it coming? If the pressure was coming from an external source, who was it? What kind of pressure could bring this kind of result?

Now my little pea-sized brain was whirling as I tried to understand what was happening to the teacher complaint at the SBEC. I was beginning to fully understand that the deck was stacked against me. And now the district's new interim executive director for human resources was joining in the fray.

He was quickly looking to review and overturn the original recommendation of the review committee. On September 22 he requested that the teacher's high school principal review all of his actions and report what he had done to investigate the parents' complaints. This was the first of three subsequent attempts made by the district to revisit the original review committee's investigation. I can only presume they were hoping for a different outcome. Isn't that the definition of insanity?

That day my attorney said it was time to get serious about protecting myself and filing a lawsuit against the Board of Trustees and the superintendent, because it was apparent that nothing I could do or say to the board or to the SBEC was going to make any difference.

So, on that same day, my attorney filed a lawsuit in federal court alleging violations of my civil rights under the First and Fourteenth Amendments to the US Constitution and the Texas Whistle-Blower Act.

Now that I had filed suit in federal court, two grievances in the district, and several complaints with the SBEC, I (me and my wonderful lawyers, that is) was fighting this battle on three fronts, in the federal court system, within the district, and at the SBEC, simultaneously.

Well, well, on October 4 I was once again a major topic at a board meeting. Lawyer Jones and the board finally got around to considering my grievances and my future. That night the school board held two separately called board meetings (that's right, two called meetings, with separate agendas, held on the same night). It seems as if this could be the title of a song, something about "the rush is on." One of these meetings was a "special" meeting with only three agenda items:

> The meeting was called to order at 6:25 p.m. and a quorum was established. The Board made a public announcement that an executive session could be held for the specific purpose of discussing matters authorized by the Texas Open Meetings Act. (October 4, 1999, special meeting minutes, agenda 1)

All three action items on the agenda that night were related to me. The first item was to vote on my August 9 grievance:

> Agenda Item 1: Grievance of Dr. Robert Durrett dated August 9, 1999. Mr. Peartree made a motion to deny this grievance, seconded by Ms. Sada.
>
> Aye: Mrs. Scrivner, Ms. Dominguez, Mr. Peartree, and Ms. Sada
> No: Mr. Sanchez and Mr. Legarreta
>
> Grievance was denied.

The second agenda item was to act on my August 12 grievance. It was also denied.

The third and final item was:

> Proposed Termination of Dr. Robert Durrett. Mr. Peartree made a motion that a letter of proposed termination be sent to Dr. Durrett, seconded by Ms. Sada.
>
> Aye: Mrs. Scrivner, Ms. Dominguez, Mr. Peartree, and Ms. Sada
> No: Mr. Sanchez and Mr. Legarreta
>
> Motion passed.

The motion passed with Mr. Peartree and Mrs. Scrivner (the recipient of the efforts made by students campaigning for her) voting aye. I did have some comfort because two board members voted not to propose my termination. As I write this, I now feel a little guilty that I did not send those two gents a thank you letter. Their comments on the record in a later proceeding indicated that they were aware, despite their lack of a background in the law, that there were fundamental rights at stake protecting the decisions I made and my filing of the two complaints.

On October 7, 1999, my second "official" notification letter, dated October 6, 1999, from Blanca Dominguez, Board President, was hand-delivered, stating

> Due to the seriousness of our findings, we, the Board of Trustees, propose to terminate your term contract of employment pursuant to Board Policy DFBA (see attached A) for the reasons stated herein which constitute good cause as determined by the Board and as set forth in Regulation DFBA-R (see attached B), to wit:

1. Insubordination, which is the refusal or failure to comply with an official order or directive in violation of DFBA-R, 4; and/or

2. Failure to comply with Board Policy DHB (see attached C); and or

3. Reasons constituting good cause.

During the preparation for my Federal lawsuit, I was present at the depositions given by several sitting board members. Board Member Peartree, during his deposition, shed a little light on his reasons of nonsupport for me or rather for his vote to terminate my employment. There will be more on the lawsuit later. But here are some interesting questions and his answers from his February 8, 2000, sworn deposition. His answers also pertained to my SBEC complaints:

Q: You're not saying that Dr. Durrett did anything illegal, are you, that you know about?

A: He has winked and nodded at a whole bunch of illegal stuff that has gone by that he has just ignored that is much worse than (teacher), using school stationary to put out electioneering things and everything else.

Q: You are not saying that Dr. Durrett used school stationary?

A: No. I'm saying he has winked at it going on and being done. (Peartree, page 26)

And later:

Q: You think that Dr. Durrett had the right to make a complaint to the SBEC years ago and failed to do so? Is that your belief?

A: He should have done one on Anthony Trujillo—and he never did—if he had done his job. (Peartree, page 27)

After listening to his answers regarding what he believed I should have done regarding Mr. Trujillo, it was becoming clear to me that some board members had been wanting to find some reason or reasons to terminate my employment.

And, later in the deposition, he testified to the following:

> Q: On more than one occasion, you and Board member Dominguez have talked briefly about the (teacher) matter and Bob Durrett. Is that correct?
>
> A: Well, you know, I've testified to you when Ronda was there. I don't know if we've ever had just a conversation between the two of us. But she has been in on some conversation between the two of us. But she has been in on some conversations that I've talked about it, yes. *Ronda has really been the spark plug* in talking about that and the accusations that she felt were untrue and such. (Emphasis added) (Peartree, page 34)

Now that piece of information was somewhat enlightening! I now knew that Scrivner, a person involved in the investigation, was the "spark plug" in pushing the board to fire me. Later in his deposition he also alluded to several additional conversations with three other board members who later voted to terminate my contract.

On October 26 SBEC Attorney Jacqueline A. Strashun wrote (the teacher) after Ms. Tackett had approved my complaint for filing. She informed him of the status of my complaint and again offered him settlement opportunities. This letter was in direct contradiction of the September 10 decision of her boss, Pamela Tackett. If you are as confused by now as I was back then, I must be in good company!

The SBEC notified me on November 1 that they had accepted for action my complaint of the conduct of (teacher). Finally, I thought I had received some good news. All that remained was to get my complaint listed on the hearing docket. But with Tackett's last letter still lingering in my mind, I was not positive. I almost (almost, but not quite) felt badly about questioning the motives of the powers within the SBEC.

On November 3, 1999, Mr. Jones, the attorney for the school district board and also for (the teacher), during a meeting with his client, (the teacher), called Ms. Strashun at the SBEC requesting that she cancel the prosecution of my complaint. Ms. Strashun testified that her verbal response to Jones was:

> The request to cancel the prosecution of the (teacher) complaint and to withdraw it was denied. (Strashun deposition, item no. 17)

Just because he did not get the answer he wanted on the phone did not mean that Mr. Jones was giving up. That same day, Jones prepared a thirty-page document to Ms. Strashun requesting that the SBEC cancel the prosecution of the (teacher) complaint and to withdraw it. This thirty-page transmittal outlined many of the defenses which he and other attorneys would later use in defending the board in the whistle-blower lawsuit which I had filed. Their defenses basically boiled down to these:

1. I filed the SBEC complaint on behalf of the Superintendent, and therefore he could fire me for insubordination because I refused to withdraw it.
2. I purposely concealed that I filed the complaint.
3. There was no evidence to support the charges.
4. There was no indication in the file that the parents' complaints were spontaneous or unsolicited.

And there were many other extraneous issues.

In his nine-page cover letter for this appeal, he made some interesting and, in my opinion, misleading statements to try to bolster his clients' case (remember he was defending both the board and the accused teacher). For example, on page 2, item 1, he stated that:

> The Superintendent takes the position that the Ysleta Independent School District, acting though (sic) its agent Robert Durrett, is the complainant in the above referenced matter.

To me, the purpose of this proposition was that Vargas could claim the complaint I filed was not my complaint but a complaint filed on behalf of the district by me. As such he could withdraw it or demand I withdraw it. If this were to become the position of the SBEC, the board would be justified to fire me for insubordination; and I would not have any recourse.

(The teacher) knew who had filed the complaint. He helped clarify this point on pages 17 and 18 of his February 2000 deposition:

> Q: Did Mr. Jones point out in the conversation to the SBEC representative that the school district had made this complaint and the school district intended to withdraw it? Did that come up in the conversation?
>
> A: No, sir, I don't recall.
>
> Q: Has Mr. Jones ever said to you that this is a school district complaint and this isn't Dr. Durrett's complaint?
>
> A: I think it was the—it was in that letter that— the letter of correspondence with the state board of education.

And a later exchange went like this on page 18:

> Q: Did you conclude that the complaint was
> filed by Dr. Durrett or the school district had
> filed it against you?
> A: I think Mr. Durrett filed it on his behalf.

Item 5 of Jones's thirty-page document helps to point out the school board's behind-the-scenes involvement in attempting to protect a fellow board member's reputation. Mr. Jones stated:

> Sometime in either June or July, Dr. Vargas
> learned from a member of the Board of Trustees
> that Durrett filed a complaint with the SBEC
> seeking disciplinary action against District
> employee (teacher). Durrett concealed his con-
> duct from Superintendent Vargas.

Apparently, Mr. Jones had forgotten, did not know, or never reviewed the process for filing a complaint. He must not have been aware that a copy of my letter of notice to the superintendent, was attached to my original complaint and that *he also attached it* to this appeal letter. That was weird! He must not have reviewed the attachments before he sent them. I was now very happy that he was the counsel for the school district!

Item 7 of his letter contains another very interesting claim. It states:

> The Durrett complaint was filed without
> the knowledge of Superintendent Dr. Edward
> Lee Vargas. Upon information and belief, the
> Superintendent believes that Durrett purposely
> concealed his filing of the complaint with SBEC.

Wow, what an interesting and bold sentence, a bold statement which takes some hubris! Why? Because the final page of my complaint, which he attached to his letter, contains a *certificate of service* declaration which states in part:

> I hereby certify that a true and correct copy of this complaint has been mailed on the 30th day of June, 1999. To the following: Dr. Edward Lee Vargas, Superintendent.

I thank God that my complaint form also contained the certified mail return receipt request number.

In the opening paragraph for item 8, Jones stated:

> A continuing investigation conducted by the District's general legal counsel reveals that there is absolutely no basis whatsoever to support the charges contained in the Durrett complaint. (A little hubris! He was the general legal counsel to which he referred in his letter.)

Then in item 8.N., he began an assault on me and the integrity of my previous employees in HR:

> Specifically, the District investigation has revealed the following: The two District employees most directly involved in the investigation against (the teacher) have a demonstrated animus towards any employee whom they believe demonstrated anti-Tony Trujillo tendencies.

Recall that Trujillo was the previous superintendent who was terminated by this same board, for, among other reasons, misappropriation of district resources by using district employees in the remodeling of his home. Item 8.N. continued:

> For example, Durrett consistently refused to take disciplinary action against at least one

other District employee who admitted under oath, during the Trujillo termination proceeding, using District resources to engage directly in political activities.

If an employee, as stated above, ever knew about Trujillo unlawfully using district resources, it was unknown by me and apparently was never reported to the HR division. It was also telling, to me at least, that Jones never notified me or the HR division of this testimony after the hearing concluded. I guess it was not that important of a transgression after all.

Apparently, Jones was not confident that he would prevail with his preceding arguments; so he continued:

In the event your agency is unable to comply with the foregoing request, we wish to inform you generally of the results of our investigation into the factual background of the Durrett complaint. (Jones, page 5)

My favorite comment in the Jones request was contained in item 16, pages 7 and 8, where he stated:

Durrett's refusal was known to other senior management employees and was causing and/or had the potential of causing a diminishment of the Superintendent's ability to manage the personnel matters of the School District.

Wow, I didn't know my refusal was such a powerful statement or that it was known to other senior administrators because I never discussed it with any administrators or disclosed it in any format to anyone other than my wonderful wife, who had no contact with these administrators.

Jones's final pleas came in two of the last three paragraphs. He said:

> Dr. Vargas would deeply appreciate you discussing this matter fully with the Executive Director of your agency and that fair consideration be given to his request.

Then finally he said if the SBEC didn't withdraw the complaint, the district would:

> ...mount a vigorous defense of the charges against its employee (teacher).

This was another one of those curious statements—curious because in one instance the board's attorney was claiming that the grade inflation complaint was filed against the employee by the district *and* the district was going to provide a vigorous defense for that same employee. Go figure. It seemed clear that the board was acting on behalf of the teacher in an effort to shield their fellow board member, Scrivner, who was not charged but was implicated in the complaint.

Items 7 through 16 are also very revealing in that Jones made the following assertions:

> Durrett, after multiple requests, failed and refused to provide Superintendent Vargas with a copy of the District's investigative file.
>
> Sometime in early July 1999 Dr. Vargas requested Durrett to withdraw his complaint...
>
> Durrett failed to follow the District's policies and procedures...
>
> Durrett refused Dr. Vargas' requests in writing on August 3, 1999.
>
> Vargas requested Durrett to reconsider his decision to refuse withdrawal of the complaint...

On August 9… Durrett, without justification, excuse, or explanation, gave written notice that he would not comply with Superintendent Vargas' request.

Durrett was suspended with full pay in consequence of his unexplained act of insubordination.

Fortunately for me Jones's formal request was denied by SBEC's lawyer, Pamela Tackett.

Then:

On November 9, 1999, SBEC filed and docketed at the State office for Administrative Hearings regarding the State Board for Educator Certification versus (the teacher) as a result of a directive of the Executive Director of the State Board for Educator Certification issued on September 10, 1999. (Strashun, item 18D)

Finally, as a result of this action by the executive director of the SBEC, a hearing was going to be scheduled. I was relieved, but the good news did not last long. I guess one half-day of euphoria is long enough. At least it is better than no euphoria at all!

I could not believe what came next! On that same day, I was notified that the administrative hearing date was set for almost a year later on October 17, 2000. I thought that was a *long* time, until I received a subpoena on September 7, 2001, requesting my presence for the hearing five days later, on the 12th of September, 2001 (subpoena, Docket No. 705-99-2685).

More waiting was the order of the day. This seemed like a long time from my June 30, 1999, filing to September 12, 2001, just to get to a hearing. But it was a state agency, after all.

My premonition that I would once again be a topic on the board agenda was accurate. I received another letter of proposed termination from the board president. This seemed very weird to me because to my knowledge the board had never voted to rescind its previous vote to propose my termination. Oh, what the heck. Rules did not seem to matter to them unless they got caught.

On November 10, 1999, I was the topic of agenda item 7, and I was not surprised that it occurred very late in the day or at the short time it took for the board to make a decision to fire me:

> At 11:20 p.m., the Board recessed into Executive Session to complete consideration of item No. 7. Following reconvening at 11:30, Mr. Peartree made a motion that Dr. Durrett's employment be terminated as of this date (November 10, 1999); second was made by Mr. Portillo. Trustee Sanchez No; Trustee Legarreta No; Trustee Scrivner Yes; Trustee Dominguez Yes; Trustee Peartree Yes; Trustee Portillo Yes; Trustee Sada Yes. Motion was approved. Mr. Sanchez and Mr. Legarreta left the meeting.

I am still sorry that I never took the time to personally thank Mr. Sanchez or Mr. Legarreta for twice voting on my behalf.

The "yes" votes were based on Vargas's recommendation that I be fired for insubordination for refusing to withdraw my (teacher) complaint. Their vote was in spite of the fact that the SBEC's investigation and enforcement division had accepted both of my complaints but had not notified me of any action being taken. I did not know if the board had been informed of any SBEC decision.

I attended that November 10 board meeting. No one rose to speak on my behalf, and I was not surprised. They finally got the procedure correct when they placed my name on the agenda. I sat on the front row and was not surprised when not a single person requested to speak on my behalf. I do remember very clearly hearing the vote being taken. When the vote was completed and it was announced that the motion passed and I was fired, I stood up and walked slowly toward the back of the room grinning from ear to ear. It was a long walk because the boardroom was an old converted Furr's Cafeteria dining room. I still believed I was right, I believed that I had fulfilled all of my legal hurdles at the district level, and now I would have my day in court. I just didn't know when that day would actually arrive. At least my thoughts were that I would no longer be subjected to school board politics. As it turned out a little later, I was partially wrong.

Mr. Jones kept churning away at those legal petitions attempting to put a stop to the SBEC process. On December 7, 1999, he prepared a document (*respondent's original answer*) for the accused teacher to be submitted to the SBEC. It contained the following statements:

> Respondent denies that he offered students grade points in exchange for their agreement to campaign for two candidates of *Respondent's choice* for the District's contested election. (Page 2)
>
> Respondent denies that he offered to enhance students' grades to perform these activities during regular school hours in exchange for their participation in campaign activities for school board candidates. (Page 4)

This was a most interesting statement. As I previously mentioned, the teacher had previously submitted a handwritten statement, with the title of "Class Project," dated May 27, 1999, in which he had admitted making the offer to his classes.

Apparently, Mr. Jones was not aware that (the teacher) had previously admitted that the activity had indeed occurred as reported by the parents and as alleged in my complaint.

CHAPTER 11

A SIDE JOURNEY

At this point in the process, I had to move on, literally, as it turned out, because I had filed my lawsuit and was seeking damages. So my lawyer informed me that now I had to "mitigate the damages." In other words, I had to go get another job. My first thought was maybe he wanted me to get a job so I could make sure I could pay his fee. But that was not the case. He informed me that I had to mitigate the damages that the school district would have to pay me if I won (I never liked that "if" word). I think he probably said when we won, not if. He was a wonderful, very positive, Christian fellow.

This "mitigate the damages" issue came up during my deposition. This was one time that the district's lawyer was looking out for the district. Just in case I won, he wanted to be sure I did not get an extra nickel. The question and my answer went like this:

> Q: I'm not trying to pry into your personal affairs, but you have an obligation under the law to mitigate your damages. Consequently, I want to ask you whether or not you were offered a position that you were applying for?
> A: I accepted the position last night.

Q: Okay. Did you enter into a contract of employment, or is it going to be an employment-at-will situation?
A: It will be at will. (Durrett, page 190)

I was very lucky that I quickly got a job as the village manager for a small village in the mountains of southern New Mexico. Shortly after beginning my new job, it became apparent that the village ordinances were very antiquated and in need of many revisions and updates. While touring the village's physical plant, I noticed several non-village vehicles parked in the fire station around the three fire trucks. This three-bay building was also packed with all sorts of car parts and trash. When I inquired of the fire chief, he informed me that one of the cars in the bay was one used in stock car races. It was in various pieces. When I asked the fire chief about the other vehicles, he said the volunteers used the fire truck bays to work on their personal cars. It did not take me long to request that the non-village vehicles be removed and that the trash be cleaned up. Now the fire chief was the only paid member of the fire department, and he did not appear to take kindly to my request.

After more looking around in the fire station, I discovered that the volunteers had a "clubhouse" type of area in the loft of one of the buildings. As it turned out, they were using it as their weekend hangout. It had a large TV and a refrigerator. This started a three-month dispute between me, the chief, and the volunteers. During my review of the village ordinances, I learned that all village volunteer firemen must be residents of the village. In comparing the applications of the volunteers and their qualifications with the ordinance requirements, I discovered many did not match.

Since it was now my responsibility to follow the rules, a.k.a. the ordinances, it became necessary for me to notify all but one of them that they no longer qualified as volunteers. Once I made the announcement that any volunteer who was not a resident of the village could no longer qualify to participate as a volunteer in the fire department, things got a little testy.

This quickly became a major "item" around the village. A lot of folks gave me their unvarnished opinions because they were concerned about having enough volunteers for the fire department. However, with the help of another village employee, we had recruited a new cadre of village residents as volunteer firemen. I made sure we had a full complement of new, trained volunteers prior to notifying the unqualified volunteers.

Well, the old volunteers' responses were not exactly what I had expected. They were not only disappointed; they threatened me and the village with a lawsuit and me with other unpleasant things.

CHAPTER **12**

REVIEW COMMITTEE RECOMMENDATION

> Lord, how many are my foes! How many
> rise up against me.
> (Psalm 3:1)

January and February of 2000 proved to be very busy with the discovery process, including depositions of Board Members Peartree and Scrivner, Superintendent Vargas, employees of the HR division, and myself.

Once depositions of all of the principal parties were almost complete, the flurry of appeals and responses exploded. For purposes of illustrations, only some are listed below. Each one of these little pieces of paper was another expense for this little guy, "me," who believed he had the law on his side.

Even my wonderful attorneys were aware of the financial strain and pain my poor wife was experiencing each month as she paid their bill. They expressed it this way in a January 22, 2000, letter as follows:

> Obviously, we are at a financially painful time of this case. The costs of depositions and attorney time have been high. We anticipate that there will be one more full day of depositions (February 8, 2000) and involve five witnesses.

In a separate paragraph they said:

> Chris and I are aware of the financial strain of this case on you, but I want you to know that in comparison to other complex cases, we are very far along on the development of the factual and legal matters necessary to prevailing at trial.

At this point I must say I never had a doubt that my attorneys were very frugal and I never doubted that they cut every corner to save me and my sweetie every dime they could without jeopardizing my case. They were now ready to do battle in court and requested that I begin to develop an analysis of the damages that my illegal termination had caused me and my sweetie.

During this same time Vargas was also pushing for action within the district. After he hired Mr. Tafoya to replace me, he also hired a new director of safety and security, Mr. Diaz. Apparently, Vargas was still looking for ways to reverse the original review committee's recommendation regarding the teacher. On March 13, 2000, Mr. Diaz submitted a three-page *executive summary* of the review committee's file to the superintendent. This summary did not exonerate the teacher, nor did it mention board member Scrivner's involvement.

Under the heading of "Purpose," he stated:

> The purpose of this summary is to advise the superintendent on the status of the investigation on the (teacher) case.

Under the heading of "ISSUES OR CONCERNS," he said:

> The focus of my investigation is to determine if there have been any procedural violations in the original investigation of the case by M. Lionel Nava, Employee Relations, and/or the review committee.

To me it was interesting that the focus of this investigation was not on the actions of the teacher in question, but on the process used in the investigation.

During this time, I continued toiling away in the mountains of New Mexico; and my lawyers were also hard at work in El Paso cranking out new motions and responses to motions. To my surprise an unexpected twist popped up.

Not only did the appeals and responses intensify but some new lawyers hired by the board were also becoming active. On February 13, 2000, the professional corporation of *Mounce, Green, Myers, Safi,* and *Galatzan* notified the court that they had entered as:

> ...co-counsel with Luther Jones, on behalf of Defendants, Board of Trustees for the Ysleta Independent School District and Edward Lee Vargas, Individually, and in his capacity as Superintendent.

In a March 14, 2000, cover letter to me, my lawyer stated this new bunch of lawyers had entered the fray and they had filed a new set of motions. My guy's opinion was "This means, obviously, that Luther has hired these gentlemen to act as co-counsel for him in your case."

It was my lawyer's opinion that Jones might have added this new law firm as a tactic to get an independent voice to the board suggesting they might be seeking a settlement. If that was the reason, it was not evident to me!

I had no way of knowing if the first action of these new lawyers was to file a motion for leave to file an amended answer based on the thirty-nine-page executive summary (of the review committee's file) prepared by Mr. Diaz. However, it was filed two days later on March 16, 2000. My goodness, these guys worked fast I thought.

My guess is that they had already been working behind the scenes without the prior approval of the trustees.

Some strange feelings began gnawing at me, because in late March we were unable to contact Jackie Strashun, the original attorney at the SBEC who was handling my complaint. She was nowhere to be found. Now my inquiries were going unanswered. Had she been removed or reassigned? Was it because she had disagreed with her boss's reversal of her decision regarding my complaint? I didn't know, but I had to appeal that decision and get it reversed. She had supported my appeal, and now she was gone, so I wondered why.

My attorney had to do some digging to locate her, and his efforts eventually paid off. Ms. Strashun reported to him that she was no longer with the SBEC. A new attorney, Ms. Sandra Fitzpatrick, had been assigned to my case.

When the SBEC lawyer, Fitzpatrick, was contacted by my attorney on April 3, 2000, he asked her about the reversal of my teacher complaint. He reported to me that she stated her only rationale for her action was she relied on the fact I had used the district letterhead paper to type my cover letter and had signed the transmittal letter as associate superintendent. Ms. Fitzpatrick did not take any of the facts stated in the complaint into consideration in arriving at her conclusion, a fact that my attorney pointed out to her a little later. He also pointed out that Mr. Jones, the board's attorney, was also (the teacher's) attorney; therefore, a finding that the district was the complainant and I was their agent in filing the complaint defied logic. There was that old question again: "How was it possible for the district to be the complainant and be defending the accused teacher?"

News of the reversal was somewhat disheartening for me, but at least my conspiracy theory was beginning to seem a little more plausible. In fact, now I really believed that the SBEC was being greatly influenced by the teacher organizations in the state and/or by the board attorneys through their connections at the SBEC. The SBEC was agreeing with the board. So once again I had to take a deep breath and contemplate what to do next.

Now the legal wrangling really got underway. You know, more lawyers mean more appeals, and more appeals mean more paperwork and more legal fees for me. It became more expensive to this ex-employee and to the taxpayers. Because the board's budget was just a little bigger than mine, they might have thought I would give up and go away. If that was their belief, they soon found out they were wrong. My wonderful wife still had a job, and she was in total support of me and my efforts.

Federal District Court Judge Harry Lee Hudspeth gave me some really good news on April 12, 2000, when he denied the board's motion for summary judgment. This was the district's second attempt to obtain a summary judgment to get out of my lawsuit. My lawyers were still butting heads with two separate law firms and the old board lawyer, Jones. That old time clock just kept on ticking for all of the lawyers involved.

The judge included one cute phrase in his April 12, 2000, *order denying defendants' motion for leave to file second amended answer* (now that is a legal mouthful). On page 5 he stated, "Recess is over, the bell has rung, and it is time to go forward with the trial."

Also in dealing with the same motion, the judge said on page 3:

> As an initial matter, the court finds that Defendants' delay in filing their motion for leave was excessive. Although Defendant Vargas may have delayed responding to Plaintiff's amended complaint out of a presumption that the case would be disposed of through his summary judgment motion, such a presumption was unjustified. Further, it does not explain why Defendant Board waited four months to respond.

And on page 5, he stated:

> In addition, the fact that Defendants have recruited new lawyers fails to adequately explain the delay, except to show a potential source for a mid-stream shift in strategy.

Also, he stated:

> Allowing Defendants to deny important facts they previously admitted and present new affirmative defenses would prejudice Plaintiff.

I wondered, *Does that phrase really mean that it is possible for someone to admit to the facts of a case and then deny them?* I wasn't sure, but at least the judge was not going to allow it in my case.

In Judge Hudspeth's order denying defendants' motion for leave to "file a second amended answer," it appeared to me that the judge was chastising the board's multiple attorneys, Mr. Jones included, for not responding in a timely manner. That day was a huge victory and a relief for me! In his cover letter my attorney described the judge's decision this way:

> This is a big victory. The Judge has signaled that he is aware of what has been going on, and that enough is enough.

In a separate paragraph in the letter, he stated in part:

> It is surprising that the first phone call to us by Bruce Koehler inquired about the possibility of mediation. Of course, our overriding interest is to keep this case on track for a May 8, 2000, trial.

While some folks might have said "whoopee" to this news, I was in no mood to settle at this point. Now I am almost embarrassed to say I wanted retribution, almost.

My waiting was almost over—only one more month before we would be going to trial! The judge had already issued his order on April 12 and stated it was time to go forward with the trial. What could possibly go wrong?

It did not take long for the last of the new hired guns to begin pumping out more motions. On April 13, 2000, the Mounce firm entered their "defendants' objections to plaintiff's *summary judgment evidence*."

Now you know that one piece of paper from their lawyer required another piece of paper in response by my guys. On April 14, 2000, they responded with "plaintiff's response to defendants' objections to plaintiff's summary judgment evidence."

With a trial date scheduled only a month away, my spirits were still high; but I did not want to get my hopes up too high. As a Christian, Apostle Paul's words in Romans 8:28 were comforting to me when he said, "And we know that in all things God works for the good of those who love him, who have been called according to his purpose."

I was correct not to get my hopes up. The board's lawyers continued to keep the delay tactics going by filing their motion on April 14. In this motion they were objecting to one of my expert witnesses. I wondered if my lawyers passed the board's lawyers in the hall as they were heading to the judge's chambers to file their motions.

Based on that April 12 ruling, my lawyer's assumption that the judge had had enough was correct. In his cover letter to me, my lawyer said, "This is ridiculous, and we tried to let the judge know just that." On the 14th he entered our response in which he stated:

In the last thirty days, Defendants have filed:

1. Defendants' motion for leave to File Amended Answer, 3/16/00;
2. Defendants' Motion to Dismiss, 3/23/00, and Defendants' Reply to Plaintiff's Response, 4/3/00;
3. Defendants' Motion for Summary Judgment, 3/23/00, and Defendants' Reply to Plaintiff's Response, 4/12/00;
4. Defendants' Motion to Exclude the Testimony of Plaintiff's Expert Rodric B. Schoen; and
5. Defendants' Objections to Plaintiff's Summary Judgment Evidence, 4/13/00.

My response to item 1 above was the same as we stated on April 12 that the amended answer would substantially prejudice my case for the following reason:

(1) the second amended answer contains several denials of facts to which Defendants had

previously admitted and upon which Plaintiff had relied in preparing for trial.

Continuing, he stated in part:

> Not one of these pleadings have meaningfully moved this matter forward toward a resolution. For example: (1) Defendants' challenge to Professor Schoen's anticipated expert testimony has been made without even testing his testimony on cross-examination in a deposition; (2) in their most recent pleading, Defendants again object to Professor Schoen's affidavit (although not his Opinion Memorandum)...

In conclusion, he stated:

> Plaintiff requests the Court overrule Defendants' Objections to Plaintiff's Summary Judgment evidence, and deny all of Defendants' pending motions.

More good news in my lawsuit! On April 18, 2000, Judge Hudspeth, in the Western District of the United States District Court, reiterated my claims of violations of my right to freedom of speech and to petition the government for redress of grievances under the First and Fourteenth Amendments. In addition, he included the fact that I was suing the board and Vargas for violations of the Texas Whistle-Blower Act. The district and Vargas had raised six separate issues in their defense of my allegations.

That day, April 18, 2000, the judge ruled as follows on three of their four motions before him. They were:

> It is therefore ORDERED that Defendants' motion for summary judgment with relation to Plaintiff's claims under the First Amendment to

the United States Constitution be, and they are hereby, DENIED.

It is further ORDERED that Defendants' motion for summary judgment with relation to Plaintiff's claims under the Texas Whistle-Blower Act for pre-suspension adverse personnel actions and suspension with pay be, and it is hereby, DENIED.

It is further ORDERED that in all other respects Defendants' motion for summary judgment be, and they are hereby, DENIED.

I thought that the judge had put the last remaining issues to rest that day when he denied the defendants' *order regarding defendants' motions for summary judgment.*

Good news! I now believed that the decisions made by the judge in my lawsuit would also impact my SBEC complaints. Finally, it seemed to me that after all the motions and counter-motions that had been ruled upon, things were headed to closure in my favor. Silly, silly me! *Somehow these decisions would be either neglected or ignored at SBEC.*

The board's attorneys now began focusing more on my lawsuit and trying every angle they could dream up to derail it. Because the board had recruited new lawyers for this appeal, my lawyers thought it seemed to indicate a potential source for a midstream shift in the board's strategy.

So I was wrong again; and I was not ready for the next surprise from the board's legal teams. In another attempt to delay my trial date, one of the district's law firms filed a request for an order staying proceedings (to delay the trial for which a date had already been set). They appealed on April 25, 2000, only eight days before the trial was scheduled. The lawyers were trying to reverse Judge Hudspeth's decision denying Vargas's qualified immunity request. This appeal was handled by the firm of Mounce, Green, Myers, Safi, and Galatzan. (How was this possible? This was the firm that the board terminated on February 1, 2000.) They asked Judge Hudspeth to consider the following *order staying proceedings*:

Defendant Edward Lee Vargas ("Vargas") is appealing the Court's denial of his qualified immunity defense from the Order Regarding Defendants' Motions for Summary Judgment entered on April 18, 2000.

Here we go again! The judge granted their stay request stating:

It is therefore ORDERED that all proceedings in the above-styled and numbered cause be, and they are hereby, STAYED pending resolution of Defendant Edward Lee Vargas's appeal to the United States Court of Appeals for the Fifth Circuit.

On page 3 of his ruling, the judge noted:

The Court recognizes that the parties are basically ready for trial scheduled in two weeks' time (as evidenced by the recently-submitted pre-trial order), and that the appellate process can be notoriously slow. While this argument is "appealing" for practical reasons, it overlooks the "right to be tried" policy that led the Supreme Court to extend the collateral order doctrine to qualified immunity cases.

It is therefore ORDERED that all proceedings in the above-styled and numbered cause be, and they are hereby, STAYED pending resolution of Defendant Edward Lee Vargas's appeal to the United States Court of Appeals for the Fifth Circuit.

Their appeal was granted on this single issue. This action resulted in a small setback for my case and more waiting and wondering about the outcome.

Bummer! Even though the judge understood that we were ready for trial, he was giving the board the delay they were seeking anyway. I was very disappointed, to say the least. The federal court system time frames were now in control of my case, and there was very little my guys could do except to wait and respond to whatever the opposing counsels would come up with. That meant more expenses for me and my sweetie. And I was reminded of the old saying that it "ain't over till it's over and the fat lady sings."

The district was not deterred by the judge's April 12 decision. They were still busy looking for new ways to defeat my cause. Apparently, Mr. Diaz's review of the review committee's decision did not arrive at the decision Vargas was wanting. So Tafoya assigned Mr. Diaz to re-review the process utilized during the (teacher's) investigation and prepare a second executive summary. His second conclusion submitted on May 2, 2000, was the review committee did not follow the policies; but his Finding Number 1 had nothing to do with policy when he stated in part:

> What (the teacher) failed to do was to obtain proper approval and appropriately document the activity so as to assure that it did not create controversy.

It is also interesting to note that Mr. Diaz's conclusion did not use board policy as the basis for his findings. Instead he used a pamphlet titled *Employee Misconduct Investigation Guidelines* which were not part of the district's policies (I had prepared this pamphlet as a supplemental guide to board regulations). His conclusion was also interesting in that it did not speak to the stated purpose of his investigation which he said was to:

> ...determine if there was misconduct on the part of (the teacher) and ensure compliance with District policy in the process.

> ...The investigation conducted by Mr.
> Nava in the (teacher) case lacked thoroughness
> and completeness.

My conclusion was that his final opinion was just that, his opinion. It did not appear to be grounded on any board policy because he stated that even if (the teacher) had failed to obtain proper approval and document the activity as required by board policy, his actions were not inappropriate. It was a curious finding to say the least, and it did not buttress my case but did not negate it in any way either. However, it did make clear that the district was making every effort to discredit the basis for "the" complaint.

One might conclude that this investigation did not provide the superintendent or the new executive director for human resources with the results they were wanting because they ordered a second investigation. The approach of the next investigation switched from the procedural issues utilized by the employees involved in the original investigation to the pamphlet's suggested processes. On May 3, 2000, the executive director received another memo from the director of safety and security. He seemed to be apologizing in the first sentence when he stated:

> I need to emphasize the focus of this investigation was to investigate the process used to investigate, present, and review the facts in the alleged misconduct of (the teacher).

The SBEC folks continued to be full of surprises. It now seemed apparent that the staff working at the SBEC were not communicating with each other. They were reversing course and were denying my complaint and accepting the board's defense that I had filed my complaint on behalf of the district. It was beginning to look like Jones's persistence was going to pay off for Vargas. The question for me was: "Why?"

While we were waiting on the Fifth Circuit to rule on their request to overturn the judge's April 18, 2000, ruling, my guys continued to push to get to a final resolution. My lawyers inquired on April 21 and May 13, 2000, as to the possibility of discussing a settlement prior to the next board member election.

On June 9, 2000, the SBEC, *sua sponte* (on their own volition) based on an incorrect application of its own regulations and without legal authority or agency precedent, rescinded its November 1, 1999, determination regarding Vargas. They used the same rationale used by SBEC Attorney Fitzpatrick and the same argument Jones had been using in responding to my ongoing federal lawsuit against the board and Vargas.

In this June 9 letter accepting the revised recommendation of the November 1, 1999, SBEC decision, the executive director of the SBEC stated:

> In light of my recent review of my decision, I have determined that you filed the complaint against (the teacher) as an agent for the Ysleta Independent School District. Therefore, Dr. Vargas, as superintendent of the district, had the authority to order you to withdraw that complaint. Such request does not violate your personal rights since you did not file the complaint in your personal capacity.

After waiting seven months, she was now reviewing my complaint. My question was: *Why?*

This decision was very disappointing, to say the least. In her letter the SBEC executive director let me know I did have an option:

> Pursuant to 19 TAC 249.52, should you wish, this dismissal may be appealed by filing an appeal with me not later than 30 calendar days after receipt of this letter.

I was confused. I personally completed the complaint form. I signed the complaint form as the complainant, but for some reason unknown to me, they did not believe I was the complainant. Hmm? Once again it seemed as if I was on my own and would not be getting any help from the agency tasked to investigate TWBA complaints.

My only recourse at this point was to launch an appeal, which my lawyers did on July 1, 2000. All I could do was wait, to which I had become accustomed.

How many successful whistle-blowers do you know? I am sure I have heard of at least one. Nope, I don't remember of one either.

Now I was sure I knew why potential whistle-blowers would rather fold than blow the whistle. It doesn't matter what you want to believe. *Like it or not, you are on your own.*

It was now apparent that the SBEC was not going to actively investigate my complaints against Dr. Vargas. As a matter of fact, they had just given Vargas the rationale to make my termination legal. This whistle-blower was positive he was now on his own. Anyone watching my situation would know that just because a state whistle-blower statute exists does not mean you have the protection of the folks charged to oversee its implementation.

Now I really questioned why I had refused to withdraw my complaint! My costs were mounting; and not only was the SBEC of no help to me but they were joining hands with the district—a "kum ba yah" moment for my adversaries.

This ruling, if let stand, would result in giving Vargas the authority to order me to withdraw my complaint and render my refusal as insubordination; and it would also legitimize my suspension and termination. Oh boy, it was time to worry.

The very agency which I believed was supposed to accept and to investigate code of ethics complaints seemed to be doing everything in their power to stifle my complaint. The SBEC appeared to be solidly in the camp of the individual accused of violating the code of ethics.

As previously mentioned, the school board was changing legal representation faster than some guys change the oil in their cars. Because of these changes, the Mounce, Green, and Myers firm requested an extension of time in the legal proceedings because they had only recently entered as co-counsel. My guys responded to them on June 16, 2000, as follows:

I received your request for an extension
and am frankly disappointed. I sought to avoid
this very problem by initiating inquiries to you
and to the Acosta firm on this very subject of
representation.

The reality of the confusion at the SBEC hit me when SBEC
Attorney Fitzpatrick sent me a detailed letter on June 27, 2000,
addressed to my old office, requesting a great deal of additional information and records which I no longer had access to. This request
was presumably to rebut (the teacher's) responses. My confusion did
not get any better! This request came eighteen days after her boss
had denied my complaint against the teacher and my appeal had not
been heard by the appeals panel. Oh, well!

As things progressed, some very interesting twists and turns
began to evolve weaving a strange web of interactions. I kept reminding myself that Fitzpatrick was the same SBEC attorney who drafted
the November 1, 1999, reversal. Now she was notifying me that she
would be prosecuting the (teacher) complaint which her boss had
recently denied. Go figure! If the twists and turns of this case were
designed into a highway, you would be able to read your own license
plate as you rounded the curves.

I was still wondering what or who influenced anyone at the
SBEC to revisit either of my complaints after a decision had already
been rendered. Did someone at Ysleta Independent School District
(YISD) pressure someone at the SBEC to review my complaints?
Was some pressure applied by the attorneys for the district? I can
only surmise. I continued to wonder because ex-SBEC attorney, Ms.
Strashun, testified in a later deposition that:

>...from November 3, 1999, and thereaf-
>ter she had numerous conversations and writ-
>ten communications with the District's lawyer,
>Luther Jones, in regards to this matter.

But now she was no longer at the SBEC, so she was not involved. She was no help in identifying the pressure point.

My concern persisted that, if this reversal was allowed to stand, it would serve as the predicate for also reversing my first complaint involving the teacher and serve as a basis for my termination for insubordination. The SBEC executive director made it perfectly clear in her June 9, 2000, letter.

My attorney had the same concern and appealed the SBEC's June 9 decision on July 5, 2000. Their response to the SBEC was quite lengthy. Thankfully a federal judge had previously ruled that my complaint was indeed my complaint, as an individual, not the district's. Here are some excerpts, contained in the judge's ruling on April 18, 2000, which were attached:

> ...the Honorable Harry Lee Hudspeth, United States District Judge, sitting in the Western District of Texas, El Paso Division, determined that there is no distinction in the law between the personal capacity and public employment of Dr. Durrett to the (teacher) Complaint that Dr. Durrett had filed with the SBEC. For that reason and for equally compelling reasons founded directly on the SBEC's Administrative Code provisions, this appeal should be granted.

My appeal letter also stated that the SBEC's decision was in direct contradiction to Judge Hudspeth's ruling which stated:

> The analysis of the SBEC, through its staff attorney Sandra Fitzpatrick, demonstrates a haphazard approach to these matters and little attention to detail. Ms. Fitzpatrick has given notice that she is the attorney who has been assigned the SBEC v. (the teacher) administrative action via her letter of June 27, 1999, to Dr. Durrett. Thus, the very attorney who crafted the recent

decision of the Executive Director of the SBEC rescinding the SBEC's approval of Dr. Durrett's complaint against Dr. Vargas and who stated that Dr. Durrett's rights were not violated when he was suspended, retaliated against, and ultimately terminated for his refusal to withdraw the (the teacher) Compliant *is the prosecutor for the SBEC on the (teacher) Complaint.* (Emphasis added)

From the beginning of my complaint to the SBEC, the district's lawyer was representing both the district and the teacher—a relationship which I believed was not only illogical but illegal and should not stand. I was not alone in my thinking. On July 10, 2000, the Delgado, Acosta, Braden, and Jones law firm, representing the district, notified the teacher by letter of their belief that a change in his legal representation before the SBEC would be necessary. The pertinent paragraph stated:

> After receiving a briefing from Mr. Jones regarding the nature of this matter, I have concerns regarding potential conflicts which may result from our representation of the Board and yourself considering other pending litigation involving substantially the same parties and operative facts.

The letter continued:

> I do not anticipate that we will be authorized by the Board of Education to continue to represent you.

On July 19, 2000, the board's attorneys filed another appeal to the US Court of Appeals for the Fifth Circuit of Judge Hudspeth's rulings—more delays, more costs, and more mental gymnastics for me.

In August of 2000 we were still waiting on the Fifth Circuit to issue a final ruling so my case could proceed to trial. The word of the day was wait, wait, and wait.

If I thought that my case was having a hard time making any headway, at least I could take heart that the Board of Trustees was also having trouble getting things moving. They were having trouble even discussing regular agenda items. On August 2, 2000, agenda item no. 3 created a lot of discussion. The minutes of that meeting showed that a point of order was called for five times. I wondered if they were having growing feelings of doubt about the recommendations they were receiving from Dr. Vargas and/or Mr. Jones.

In the midst of the board's disarray, I received great news from the executive director of the SBEC. My lawyer expressed it this way in his letter to me:

> As you can see, the appeals panel REVERSED Pamela Tackett's decision to dismiss the complaint. Congratulations, big guy.

In her letter of August 9, 2000, she reported to me that on August 1, 2000, the committee panel reversed the executive director's (her) dismissals relating to principle 3, standard 6; principle 3, standard 7; and principle 2, standard 5. She also stated:

> In accordance to the Committee Panel ruling, a petition on behalf of the complainant containing the Code of Ethics violations mentioned will be filed with the State Office of Administrative Hearings.

She did not mention that my appeal was upheld by a unanimous vote of the committee panel, but she did include a copy of their vote. That paragraph put a smile on my face!

The regular board meeting on August 9, 2000, dealt not only with the conflict of interest of Mr. Jones representing the (teacher) and the board before the SBEC but many other management issues.

The closed session agenda item no. 6 and governance action item A for that night included:

> Discuss proposed action to retain and authorize the District's special counsel, Law Offices of Victor H. Falvey, to conduct an investigation of Dr. Edward Lee Vargas, Superintendent of Education, regarding...violations of State law...employing persons to fill vacant positions without advertising as required by Board policy; violations of Board policy with respect to employee investigations and reports to the Board of Trustees, obligating the District to pay legal expenses for an attorney not retained by the Board of Trustees;...

Apparently, the board was now beginning to understand what some of my concerns were when I filed my SBEC complaint against Vargas. There were many other specific items listed for investigation, but the two mentioned above were duplicates of charges in my grievances. They were:

> ...employing persons to fill vacant positions without advertising as required by Board policy; ...violation of Board policy with regard to employee investigations and reports to the Board of Trustees.

One other item in the motion that was also of interest to me was:

> ...obligating the District to pay legal expenses for an attorney not retained by the Board of Trustees...

Apparently, this item referred to the motion which they previously passed on February 1, 2000, to retroactively pay for fees incurred without their authorization. The motion passed.

In my opinion, the next motion was on target; and it gave me some hope that maybe, just maybe, justice would eventually be done:

> Trustee Sanchez made a motion that Dr. Vargas be suspended pending the litigation that has been indicated in Item A.

The motion passed. Now I did not shout out "hallelujah" when I heard this news, but I must admit that I was not displeased.

Because I was footing the bill for my attorneys, I must say I was pleased with item no. 5 of that same board agenda. On August 9, 2000, the board considered whether they would authorize payment to attorneys representing (the teacher) before the SBEC. The motion stated:

> Consider and take appropriate action on State Board for Educator Certification v. (the teacher)...based on July 10, 2000, letter from law firm...and provide direction to attorneys as discussed in Closed Session... Trustee Sanchez made a motion to instruct our legal counsel that since the District's legal counsel has a conflict of interest that the District not provide legal counsel for this man, Seconded by Trustee Lerma... Motion was approved.

It was interesting to me that Trustee Peartree voted along with Trustee Scrivner because of her involvement in the grade inflation campaign issue. They were the only trustees to vote "no," which meant they wanted to continue to pay attorneys' fees for the alleged perpetrator.

At the pace the board was hiring attorneys, I was beginning to wonder how much money they were willing to spend just so they would no longer have to look at my big floppy ears. Because new law firms were being involved, I could only assume that Jones was now mainly focusing on my SBEC complaints regarding the teacher and Vargas or he was over his head regarding my lawsuit and needed assistance.

It was the Delgado law firm which raised concerns about Mr. Jones representing both the teacher and the board because of Jones's potential conflict of interest. This change in representation was reported to the SBEC on August 10, 2000. In their letter they stated it this way:

> Last evening the Board took up the matter and elected not to authorize funding for the defense of (the teacher).
>
> Therefore, the Board of Trustees will not be providing a lawyer to represent (the teacher) in this matter.

That same day, August 10, 2000, the Delgado firm also notified Mr. Kerry Sullivan, State Administrative Hearing Office, Austin, Texas, that:

> This is a report made pursuant to Your Honor's request regarding the action of the Board of Trustees of the Ysleta Independent School District as to whether the District will provide an attorney and defense for (the teacher) in the captioned matter. Last evening the Board took up the matter and elected not to authorize funding for the defense of (the teacher).

The August 17, 2000, issue of the *El Paso Times* reported on the state's continuing investigation concerning Dr. Vargas's administrator certification. The article stated in part:

> The investigation involves the firing of an associate superintendent... The Texas State Board for Educator Certification will file a petition within 50 days to the state Office of Administrative Hearings in Austin, calling for a trial-like hearing on violations of the state's code of ethics, board spokesman Brad Ritter said.
>
> The investigation involves the firing of Robert Durrett, former Ysleta associate superintendent of human resources, by Vargas and the Board last year.

Another interesting item (to me at least) was on the August 23, 2000, board agenda. Agenda item no. 9 was to replace the attorney previously hired on August 9, 2000, to investigate the allegations against Vargas with a new law firm. I guess bigger is better when you are hiring lawyers and law firms.

The last item on the agenda that night was a funny one to me. It was becoming very apparent that the Board of Trustees was having a tough time getting along. Item no. 13 made it clear to all that it was not a "kum ba yah" time. The motion was to:

> Approve the resignation of the entire Board of Trustees, with individual resignations to be valid only if all seven trustees resign.

Even this motion failed on a split vote.

By now even the board apparently knew they had become so fractured that outside intervention was needed. So on August 28, 2000, they voted to:

> Discuss and take action requesting that a Texas Education Agency Master be assigned to the Ysleta Independent School District.

The motion was approved, once again, on a split vote.

On September 14, 2000, I received yet another surprise from the SBEC. After reviewing the complaint and the SBEC file on (the teacher), Ms. Fitzpatrick wrote Superintendent Vargas and requested the district provide her with the entire investigative files on (the teacher). She stated in part:

> This agency has filed a code of ethics complaint against (the teacher) as relates to his involvement with soliciting students in 1999 during the performance of his duties as a government teacher to work in the school board campaigns of Ms. X and Mrs. Scrivner.

While reading her letter, I noticed that she referred to (the teacher) as a government teacher. I kept wondering where she picked up on the fact that (the teacher) was a government teacher. The information was nowhere to be found on my official complaint document or in any of my communications. Maybe they had actually looked at his file in their office.

On October 4, 2000, the district sent the entire (teacher) file to Ms. Fitzpatrick at the SBEC. I can only surmise what might have been discussed among the YISD board and Vargas wondering why or what caused the SBEC to reverse their original decision.

During the process someone in the district must have been concerned about my winning my lawsuit because Vargas and/or Jones had hired a bunch of lawyers. A curious point about one of the hirings was that the board's motion to approve their work was for *retroactive* approval. In fact, it was for work performed eight months before they were authorized to work. The motion on October 23, 2000, was to:

> Approve an engagement letter effective February 1, 2000, with Mounce, Green, Myers, Safi & Galatzan for work referred by Luther Jones and/or Dr. Edward Lee Vargas. (Page 27,

consent agenda, item 18, special board meeting, October 23, 2000)

I am not an attorney, but I am pretty sure that it was not legal to approve a contract to "hire someone" after the work had already been performed. A board member apparently agreed and pulled the item. At that point I was aware that their work involved my lawsuit.

Then the board's attorney, Jones, on November 3, 2000, again requested that the SBEC cancel the prosecution of the (teacher) complaint. Ms. Strashun, SBEC attorney, reported that his request was denied and my complaint was scheduled for a hearing on November 9, 2000 (Strashun, page 5).

I am such a slow learner! It finally dawned on me that now Board Member Scrivner might have been concerned about the outcome of my SBEC complaints and my lawsuit *because*, as previously stated, she was also a certified educator and was employed in a neighboring school district. Consequently, any penalty enforced against (the teacher) might also apply to her because she was the recipient of the students' efforts. I have no clue as to whether or not she was concerned or whether or not she shared this potential concern with other board members.

My belief that whistle-blowers are on their own seemed to be confirmed on March 15, 2001, when the *El Paso Times* reporter Gustavo Reveles Acosta reported the following:

> The State Board of Educator Certification stopped an investigation into allegations that Vargas wrongfully fired former associate superintendent Robert Durrett. A decision against Vargas could have cost him his license to work in Texas. "This was an agreement between our legal staff and (Vargas') lawyers," state board spokesman Patrick Shaughnessy said. "It can be brought up again, but right now it is on the back burner."

This little report did not heighten my spirits!

CHAPTER 13

PRIOR EMPLOYMENT EXPERIENCES

My trouble at the district was not the first time I had been fired as an adult. I had *been there and done that* once before. However, the circumstances were quite different.

The other time was for being too efficient. I know that seems impossible for me at this point but, yes, doing too good of a job. Well, fired is a little misleading; my position was eliminated. One of my majors in college was finance. When I was employed as a credit adjustor for Central Bank and Trust in Denver, Colorado, one of our customers, "Brownie" of Western Mobile Homes, Inc., recruited me to be his finance manager. He had a portfolio of several million dollars in accounts receivable. It was a fun job; the company had six sales lots around Colorado. The company had a six- seat airplane, and Brownie was an excellent pilot. We would make regular trips to the sales lots each month.

Now flying was kind of like my traveling squad experience in high school because previously the only "flight" I had taken was in a helicopter ride from where I was stationed at a missile site in Los Angeles to and from Fort MacArthur. I loved flying with him. After going to work and analyzing the company's accounts receivables, which I should have done prior to accepting the position, I determined that he was losing money every month and he should sell the receivables accounts. He saw the wisdom in my recommendations; and, uh-oh, he no longer needed a finance manager. I guess I should have thought about that before I made that recommendation. Being a small independent mobile home dealer, he did not have extra cash to pay me for just sitting around doing nothing. However, he was very gracious; and he gave me a two-week notice with pay; and he also gave me an alternative. He offered me a sales position on one of the sales lots, which I declined because I had heard too many stories from the sales staff.

This was another lesson in life, that is, following the rules and doing a good job does not always lead to happy endings. It can lead to unintended consequences, some good and some not so good. However, in the long run I also benefitted from this experience. But it was in the long run before I realized that I had indeed benefitted.

At that time I had two young kids and a wife and was now unemployed and looking for a job. This was the only time I had ever used a state employment service to look for a job, but I only had two weeks; and it was free. It proved fruitful. Two weeks later I was the assistant credit manager for a Woolco Department Store in Westminster, Colorado.

A couple of years later, Woolco's corporate finance vice president (VP) transferred me to Houston, Texas, where Woolco was opening seven new stores. In order to open the stores with a large base of customers, the corporate office issued thousands of credit cards. Unfortunately, many of the card holders were less than stellar credit risks and, in my opinion, should never have received a credit card. It was also my opinion that the corporate officers did not follow the basic rules of the lending industry. Delinquency rates began to rise, and it became impossible for me to reduce the store's payment delinquency rate. But for me it did reinforce the concept that most rules exist for a reason and are to be followed because they usually lead to the desired outcome. It became apparent to me that, even in the corporate world, you should do your homework and be cautious when you deviate from the rules.

Being transferred to Houston was not the best move we had made. Neither I nor my wife was happy in Houston. The weather was hot and humid most of the time, and I was working six days a week. My first and only Christmas Eve at the store was a real doozy. We were scheduled to close the store at 10:00 p.m., but when ten rolled around the store was packed. The assistant manager announced that shoppers needed to stop shopping and get to the registers and check out. That little blurb on the intercom brought very little response. So we waited and waited. Finally, at eleven thirty he made another quick announcement that the registers were closed, shut off the lights except for the emergency lights, and said everyone should exit the building because security would be at the front door because no one would be allowed to take any merchandise out of the store. The sounds that erupted from the remaining customers were less than pleasant, but we finally got to go home.

Our dislike of the weather in Houston, my frustration with the store, and our general circumstances led me to begin a search for other employment opportunities. I thought a return to college and getting a master's degree would broaden my employment options, so I applied for a position at Eastern New Mexico University (ENMU), my old university. God was so good to me. He was there with me when they opened the door for me and offered me an interview the next week. Mr. Rasmussen, my eventual boss, even agreed to interview me the next Saturday. So I left Houston late on Friday night and drove all night from Houston to Portales, New Mexico, was interviewed late Saturday afternoon, and returned to Houston on Sunday. Mr. Rasmussen called me on Monday and offered me the job, which I accepted. On Monday I resigned, gave my two weeks' notice, and got back to Portales and ENMU.

While at ENMU I was blessed with several administrative positions. Originally, I was hired as the director of community services. My major function was to contact area communities, perform an analysis of their juvenile delinquency issues, and develop delinquency prevention programs unique to local issues identified by each community. The topic seemed fitting for me because of my own personal juvenile experiences which I could draw from to assist the local city councils. Part of the program included developing juvenile (peer) courts made up solely of juveniles. Their function was to develop and enforce their specific local rules for conduct. The peer jurors were allowed to develop the consequences, within reason, for *not following the rules.*

During my sixteen years of employment with the university, I was promoted to assistant to the president where I served two presidents and three interim presidents before being tasked to create the office of personnel. Now, I not only had to *follow the rules but* was tasked to create them, publish them, and administer them.

As assistant to the president of ENMU, I was also the recording secretary for the university's foundation. At one meeting the foundation board asked me to retrieve the foundation's checkbook which was maintained by the vice president of finance. When I made the request, he said it was not in his office and the board could not have access to it anyway. When I reported back to the foundation board, they were startled at his response and, after much discussion, decided to simply report the situation to the university Board of Regents.

Coincidently, during that same day, an accountant, Robert (Bob) Bleakley, was working in the business office, attempting to close the construction account on the recently completed Greyhound Arena. Bob pulled me aside and explained that he could not account for a twenty thousand-dollar refund check from the contractor, and it appeared to him that the vice president of finance had transferred that check to a personal account. I instructed Bleakley to sequester all of his paperwork, call the state auditor's office, explain what he believed to be the situation, and request an immediate audit. After calling the state auditor, Bob asked if he could stay out of the office until the auditor arrived; so I sent him home. It's not that I had that authority, but it seemed like a good idea at the time.

Once the state auditor arrived, it was a short time before the vice president was confronted with the twenty thousand-dollar discrepancy. It did not take long before he confessed to embezzling that check and much more. He eventually confessed to embezzling over 230,000 dollars. He was subsequently sentenced to a two-year prison term. It was later determined that he had actually embezzled more than 250,000 dollars over the previous seven years.

The VP had developed an ingenious plan to divert funds from a lease agreement with the US Post Office. He later stated that the

US Postal Service (USPS) would not enter into an agreement with the university because they required a person's name on the lease. So he signed the agreement which leased a portion of Lea Hall to the USPS.

Consequently, the checks for the lease came to his office and were made out to him as the payee. It became apparent that he devised his plan during the first negotiations with the USPS, because starting with the first rental check he deposited the checks in his personal checking account. This discrepancy was not discovered until the state auditor began his investigation of the non-related construction account. His ruse was actually uncovered by the VP's secretary who had *followed the rules*. She had always opened the mail and made copies of every check received in the business office's mail before passing the checks on to the VP for review. He would remove the checks made out to him from the USPS and return the remaining checks to an accountant for deposit.

Apparently, he was not aware that his secretary had been making copies of all checks for the past ten or twelve years. As it turned out, his little ruse proved to be a pretty good deal for about seven years. I later read a book on embezzlers which described his personality perfectly. The book described embezzlers as nice guys, likable, and always aiming to please whomever they dealt with. And indeed he was a really nice guy. He was liked by almost everyone and considered a pillar of the community. This was a very difficult situation for me because I really liked him and could not believe what was happening. As a side note, when he was paroled, he called me to apologize for what he had done.

CHAPTER 14

PUBLIC SERVICE

During my adult years in Portales, I was elected to two four-year terms on the city council (after losing my first election attempt by twenty-four votes). One of the great joys of this experience happened the night before my first victory. It was late that Monday night when the phone rang. I will never forget that call. When I answered the phone, this very soft frail voice said, "This is Ms. Lillian. Are you my Bobbie Durrett?" I could not believe it! This was my first first grade teacher (that is correct; you may recall that I did not make it through the first grade the first time). This was the same teacher who had bent my hands backward and busted wooden rulers over my palms and put tape over my mouth because I was talking too much in class. I am sure I deserved every piece of tape, every broken ruler, and every kind of discipline she could dish out. When I said, "Yes, it is," she responded, "I just wanted to make sure you were my Bobbie Durrett because I wanted to vote for you tomorrow because you were such a sweet boy."

Now, I will never say she had a bad memory; I will only say she must have only remembered my freckled face, cute smile, and floppy ears. I was blown away!

I believe every citizen should be forced to serve on some elected body. (I guess that wouldn't make it elective, would it?) Being forced to vote your conscience and be accountable to someone else can be a humbling experience. The best experience I had was serving with council members I respected and considered friends and who were honorable. That does not mean we always agreed with each other; it simply means we worked together with no animus toward each other when we disagreed. Thirty years later we are still friends.

My second most memorable council-related experience was when the Southwest Voters Rights League from San Antonio, Texas, sued the city for discrimination. At that time all city council seats were elected at-large by the popular votes of all the votes cast. The remedy sought by the league was for our little city of ten thousand to go from at-large elections to elections by single-member districts. During my deposition on that lawsuit, the only question I remember being asked was something like this: "The city of Albuquerque has a population of one hundred thousand, and they elect their city council members by single-member districts. Don't you agree that that is a better way to elect representatives?" My response was something like "Let's see. We have eight council members representing ten thousand people; and they have one person representing ten thousand constituents; so I guess our representation is about eight times better." That was the last question I remember being asked. I was a little disappointed several years later when the council decided to settle the case. However, I did understand. It was and is very costly for a small town to shell out legal fees over the differences of opinions on how to elect representatives. But, in my opinion, single-member districts bring about a "my constituents" versus "your constituents" attitude instead of what is good for the whole.

Following the rules also popped up in a different way while I was serving on the city council. It forced me make the choice either to follow the rules, bend them, or refuse to enforce them to protect a friend.

I was the chairman of the city council's personnel subcommittee. One heart-wrenching issue I had to deal with involved a friend, my vote, and members of my Sunday school class. The personnel subcommittee received a complaint regarding a city employee. The allegations were that he was using his assigned city vehicle to travel to another city for nefarious activities. He was married to a friend I had known since the first grade. (No, I don't remember if she was a

friend from my first or second attempt at first grade.) At the completion of the investigation, the allegations were found to be true. The
committee recommended that the employee be allowed to resign if
he wished and, if not, he could request a hearing before the council.
Also, if he chose to have a hearing, he could choose to have an open
or a closed hearing.

At the urging of some of our mutual friends, he chose to request
an open hearing. Of course, this was big news in our small town. The
council was required to publish notices of the hearing in the local
newspaper. The employee and his wife had many friends in town,
many of whom were in my Sunday school class. One afternoon several members of that class came to my office. They told me what a
good man the individual was and demanded that I move to cancel
the hearing. They berated me for allowing such a thing to happen to
such a fine fellow. I thought about asking or begging them to talk
to our friend and ask him to resign. By now, my stubbornness was
taking over. I did plead with them to give me as much respect as they
gave to him. I guess I must not have been very convincing because
they left my office in a huff.

Well, the hearing went off as scheduled; the dirty laundry was
out in the public for all to see and hear. The decision of the council
was termination. My Sunday school buddies never did apologize.

However, one more time I did follow the rules, even though the
results were personally disappointing.

CHAPTER 15

INTO THE FRAY

After sixteen years at ENMU, I was beginning to feel the need to seek new opportunities and move on. For several years I had been driving to Lubbock, Texas, and attending graduate school at Texas Tech. Now I had completed all of my coursework and only needed to prepare a dissertation to complete an Ed. D. degree. I would no longer need to be close to Lubbock to attend classes, so I began searching for a new job. When I accepted a position with the University of Texas in El Paso (UTEP), Texas, I resigned from my position at ENMU and my city council seat.

After three years at UTEP as director of personnel, I was promoted to assistant vice president of business affairs. After 5 years at UTEP I applied to and was hired by the Ysleta Independent School District in El Paso as associate superintendent for human resources. This proved to be the last position I would occupy in the field of education.

At this point in my career, I did not have to decide if I had to follow the rules; it was now just a part of whom I had become. *The "following rules" thing now seemed to be embedded in my psyche.*

I had worked hard all of my life to achieve what I believed to be a very responsible position. As the associate superintendent for human resources, my decisions and/or recommendations could impact the education of over fifty thousand students and the lives of over eight thousand employees. After working almost 10 years in the district, my ego said I could, and I believed I had made a positive difference during my employment with the district. After my arrival we had progressed from a low-performing district to a "recognized district."

I did, however, receive an early wake-up call when I arrived at the district. Following district policy did not seem to be of utmost importance to the district's senior administrators prior to my appointment. It had previously been common practice for a campus principal to request a transfer of a teacher for any reason or no apparent reason, regardless of the circumstances. If the principal did not like a teacher, they would simply request the teacher be moved to another campus by making the request to my predecessor, who would process the paperwork without questioning the reason(s).

I had not been on the job very long when a principal sent me a request to transfer one of his teachers to another campus. I was surprised when no reason was given. Being new to the district, I was curious as to why he wanted the teacher transferred. I inquired if the teacher had requested to be transferred or if it was to be an involuntary transfer. When I was told it was an involuntary transfer, I was curious about her performance. So I asked him about her performance evaluations, and his response was that she was a good teacher. Indeed, a review of her evaluations by this principal showed he had always evaluated her as an excellent teacher. Naturally, I was curious as to why any principal would want to transfer an excellent teacher who had not requested a transfer. I continued to press him for his reasons. So when he insisted she must be transferred, I pressed him for the "real" reason(s). Finally, he said she was really not an excellent teacher and was troublesome and he had only given her good evaluations because he did not want to have any hard feelings on his campus.

When asked why he felt it was okay to transfer her and have her teach children on other campuses but not the kids on his campus, he appeared to become flustered. After some counseling on the purpose of teacher performance evaluations, I reminded him it was a process for improving the performance of our employees. Performing proper evaluations either would lead to good teaching or would document the reasons the teacher needed to seek a new line of work.

Consequently, I did not approve his transfer request. After the second such conversation with another principal, the word must have gotten around because I no longer received unfounded requests for transfers. Some principals agreed with me, and some didn't. My fan club did not appear to be growing.

CHAPTER 16

MORE REFLECTIONS ON FAMILY

Was there something embedded in me by my family that made me stubborn? I wondered and reflected.

In the summer of 1957, Dad let me drive his old dump truck to haul gravel on the road job on which he was working as the maintenance mechanic. We were working on a road job on Route 666 close to Tohatchi Indian Reservation outside of Gallup, New Mexico.

After a few weeks Mr. Les Wheeler, one of the owners, asked me to drive the oil distributor truck. I was excited because it paid more than driving for my dad. When I asked my dad, he told me to go ahead. It was much later when I learned that my dad lost a lot of money that summer when he let me drive for Les. During this summer I learned a lot about my dad. I saw him buy and sell pickups and trucks on a handshake. You could trust him to do what he said he would do regardless of the consequences. His word was his bond. This character trait is a part of his legacy which he left with me. I hope that is how most folks view me.

Late one afternoon a brand-new, bright-yellow Caterpillar D9 (Pusher Cat for the rock crusher) broke down. Les Wheeler, the general contractor, told my dad to get it fixed as soon as possible because he could not afford to have the rock crusher down. The "Pusher Cat" was used to push the larger rocks into the crusher to produce gravel for the base course of the road. Mr. Wheeler left the jobsite and headed out to the highway. So Dad proceeded to use a cutting torch to cut a big hole in the side of that brand-new, bright-yellow Cat. He had to crawl inside to get to the broken part and weld it back together.

When Mr. Wheeler arrived at the jobsite early the next morning, he came screeching to a halt in his big pink Cadillac. When he saw his new bright-yellow Cat had a large hole burned in the middle, the tracks off, and the two halves spread apart, he screamed and began spewing a blue streak of profanities. He wanted to know what in the world Dad was doing. I will never forget the look on Les's face when Dad replied, "You said you wanted it fixed now, not next week; and that is what I am doing. It will be ready in the morning." Les threw up his hands and drove away.

One evening as I was parking the oil distributor, I backed over some fifty-five-gallon oil drums and dislodged several of the sprayer lines. Dad and my brother Charlie, who was home from law school, worked most of the night to repair the lines. Because I, his son, had created the problem, Dad would not turn in his time sheet for doing these repairs. Later Charlie told me that Dad would not let him turn in his time sheet either because I was the one who damaged them. I am still amazed that Charlie didn't give me a thrashing, but I could tell he was not happy with me.

Dad was one of the smartest uneducated men I have ever known. He could repair anything mechanical. I am truly grateful for the legacy of hard work, honesty, and following-the-rules mind-set he left me and his family. It's too bad I had to leave home to appreciate him.

My oldest brother, Ed, was also an inspiration to me. He was drafted into the Navy in 1941 and became a Navy Seabee during WWII and was very proud of it. He did not like to talk about his time in the service. The only story he ever told me about while he was in the service was being on guard duty in the Philippines. One night he was carrying a Thompson submachine gun guarding the chicken coops. When they all began cackling and making very loud noises, he said he began firing at the area of the noises. When it was all over, he had shot several chickens and a very large python. After he was discharged, he returned home to Portales and went to ENMC on the GI Bill and received a BA degree, certification as teacher, and later a master's. Here he met and married a farm girl from Grady, New Mexico. I was young enough to be the ring bearer at their wedding. He wouldn't talk about WWII, but he loved to talk about the kids in his classes. During his many years of teaching elementary students, he insisted that they learn the multiplication tables before they could use a calculator during class. When a parent challenged his policy at a school board meeting, the board instructed him to let all of his students use calculators whenever they asked. He was so committed to this concept that he resigned and retired. He must have also had a little of Dad's stubbornness in him. Maybe some of my stubbornness also came from Ed.

When Ed passed away, my brother Tom and I were allowed the privilege of placing his ashes in the family plot in Portales. We had a few decisions and choices to make. Ed loved to golf, so we wanted to honor that hobby in some way. In looking around for the appropriate container, we found a beverage cooler in the shape of a golf bag that his daughter had given him. It looked like the perfect container. However, the outside was made of some kind of fabric, so we had to find something to put it in. Since we were in farming country, we headed to the local commercial sprinkler dealer in search of a piece of large PVC pipe. We wandered around the back lot and found some large pipe that would work, but it was in twenty-foot pieces. When the clerk inquired as to what we needed, we told her we needed about thirty inches of the big pipe. She quickly informed us that she could not sell us a thirty-inch piece. As we continued to look around, her boss came out to see if he could help us. When we told him we needed thirty inches of the large pipe to bury our brother's ashes, he retrieved a hacksaw, cut off what we needed, gave us plugs for each end, and said, "God bless. Take it with my blessings." I wish I could say that was the end of the story, but when we got to the cemetery, the ground was extremely hard. We struggled for a couple of hours just to dig that small hole.

A couple of weeks later, my brother got a call from the cemetery groundskeeper. Tom was informed that we had buried Ed's ashes on the wrong side of the headstone. I am sure Ed had a good laugh from the heavens above. Some twenty years later, I finally confessed to his widow. She almost could not stop laughing.

Living in Portales helped my dad realize his dream of his kids getting a college education. All of my four brothers and my younger sister, Ruth, attended ENMU. In addition to Ed's degrees mentioned earlier, Charlie attended as a prelaw major and completed his JD degree at the University of New Mexico. Tom took classes for thirteen years before completing a BA, an MBA, and then later an Ed. S. degree. Jerry received a BA. I received a BA, an MBA, and an Ed. S. from ENMU before completing an Ed. D. from Texas Tech in Lubbock. Ruth attended ENMU but did not graduate. She later became a certified legal secretary.

Even though Dad moved us to Portales because of the university, he never made a big deal about our graduations, even when five of us graduated on the same night. I; my brothers Tom and Jerry (not to be confused with the cartoon characters); my wife, Carolyn; and my brother Ed's wife, Wilma, all crossed the stage together. Dad was not going to attend our graduation ceremony because, as usual, he was working out of town. Over the years Ed, Charlie, and I had all worked for Wheeler and Trotz Construction Co., Dad's bosses at that time. We decided to call Les Wheeler and ask him to send Dad home for our graduation ceremonies, and he did. *The Amarillo Globe-News* thought it was a big deal even if Dad didn't. The *Globe-News* ran a great story and took the only photo we have of the event. The "professional" photographer we had hired "forgot" to put film in the camera. Go figure!

In all the years Charlie, Tom, and I played sports in public school, Dad only attended one of our combined sporting events. And that was only because our Uncle Shep made him go to a Thanksgiving Day game in Clovis. Charlie was playing, and Shep thought Dad should see him play. You see, Dad did not care about the "small stuff," as he called it; he only cared about results. That was why his only rule for us after we graduated from high school was to stay enrolled in college, or else. The "or else" meant that, as long as we were enrolled in college and making passing grades, he would provide us "three hots and a cot" (that is, room and board). Once we left college, for any reason, we were to get a job and get out of the house.

Dad made sure we learned what it meant to follow the rules or suffer the consequences. My personal eviction from home came after my first three semesters of partying and teaching those college professors all I knew. After my first three semesters, the dean of students requested my presence; and he advised me that I needed to take a break, grow up, and then maybe, just maybe, return "someday." That was also my unspoken eviction notice from the homeplace.

My journey through the higher education system was quite different from my brothers. I really did enjoy my first three semesters of college. Partying and doing stupid things were the order of the day for me. One example should suffice to highlight my time. One hot July evening during my freshman year, I and several of my buddies decided for our friend Jere Beasley's birthday, we should crown him the "king of the hops" with a beer party. Being the astute fellows we were, we decided to party in the local cemetery because we did not want to disturb anyone. It seemed like a good idea at the time. Once the beer was iced down in the irrigation ditch next to the gravel road, we settled in to party.

During the celebration something must have gone wrong with our noise level, because some local farmers living close to the cemetery called the sheriff. It was quite a surprise when those headlights began popping up at the various entrances to the cemetery. They quickly rounded us up and confiscated the beer we had left in the bed of the pickup. After a short greeting from the sheriff's posse, we checked in (as in "were ushered in") to the police station. Once the formalities were over, we were all released with a court date. The charge was disturbing the peace. (Now come on. Disturbing the peace in the cemetery?) After being released by the sheriff, we were determined to continue the party. So we returned to the cemetery to retrieve the beer we had previously iced down in the irrigation ditch which the sheriff had not confiscated and continued the party elsewhere.

It just so happened that during that summer my dad was working in Nara Visa, New Mexico, some 150 miles from home. It was the only time I can remember that my mom went with him to a work site. It was also the only time I can remember that I was left at home alone during a summer. So I was harassing the others guys because their parents would know we had been arrested and mine would not. Boy, was I wrong! On the day of our hearing, we were all standing at the bench facing the judge when he glanced up and said, "Yes, ma'am, may I help you?" When I turned around to see to whom the judge was talking, I saw my mother standing there, all by herself. She was the only parent in the room. What a shock! My mom did not drive and had been out of town, and here she was. She did not utter a word, sat down, and waited. When the judge issued his decree of a twenty-five-dollar fine for each of us, I turned around to see if she would help me with some cash, but she had disappeared. No help was coming from her. At that point I was reminded the last time I got into trouble, my dad told me in no uncertain terms, "If you are old enough to get yourself into trouble, you are old enough to get yourself out. Don't call me."

I suppose it was his subtle way of saying, "From now on *follow the rules or suffer the consequences.*" Now some sixty years later I still do not know how my mother, the only parent who was out of town, found out about the incident. Every time I inquired, she would just smile and walk away. My brothers claimed to be innocent, so it is still a mystery.

Five Durretts graduate from ENMU on July 31,
1964. Left to right Wilma Jean, Carolyn Jean,
Robert Duane, Thomas James and Jerry Dean.

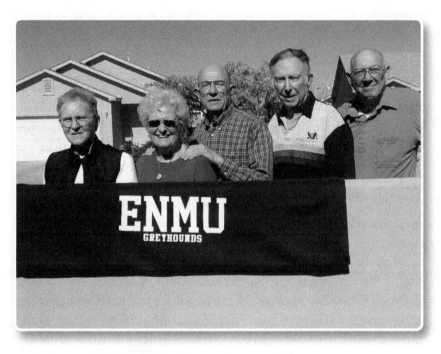

The same Durretts 50 years later in July 2014.

CHAPTER 17

GETTING TO MY LUCKIEST DAY EVER

Later, after flunking out of college, I knew I had to vacate the home-place. Now I had to look for new horizons. I had joined the National Guard between my junior and senior year in high school. Lucky for me being in the Guard created a new opportunity. I decided to volunteer and go on active duty. When I volunteered, the recruiter gave me a choice on which discipline of the Army I wanted to be trained. I selected a training program in air defense. I was to attend a Nike Ajax (antiaircraft missile) Fire Control school. There were only two locations in the United States where I could obtain the training. When I filled out my forms, my request was to go to Fort Dix, New Jersey, because I wanted to see a part of the country I had never seen. But, to my dismay, I was sent to Fort Bliss, Texas, only 150 miles from home and across the river from Juarez, Mexico, a place I had been many times. The purpose of the training was to learn how to repair the computer systems which tracked incoming airplanes and controlled the Nike Ajax target-tracking and missile-tracking radars. I learned many valuable lessons at Fort Bliss, some even about the missiles' radar system, and made some really good friends.

Being a country boy from the sand hills of New Mexico, I was still very naive about the ways of the world, so to speak. One weekend I had a seventy-two-hour pass, so I decided to return home for a short visit. Each payday we were paid cash. As soon as we got paid, I made sure I set aside enough cash to pay my bills and put it in my footlocker. I wanted to leave very early the next morning; so I laid out my civilian attire, socks, shoes, wallet, and watch on top of my footlocker. I wanted to be able to get dressed in the dark without disturbing any of the fellows in the bay area. Because we were paid in cash, my wallet contained all the spending money I had for the weekend. Much to my dismay, the next morning my wallet was missing. To say I was a little disappointed would be an understatement. I am pretty sure I went ballistic, waking everyone in the bay and using at least a few choice words, but to no avail. I never found out who the culprit was, but I did find out who my buddies were. They floated me a loan so I could get home.

Juarez, Mexico, is just a few miles from Fort Bliss. My friends and I made many weekend trips over the border to enjoy this fine city. We frequented the finest restaurants and bars. The Kentucky Club was just two blocks from the border crossing and was always our first stop—great margaritas and twenty-five-cent draft beer. Then we would go on to the Florida Club for a great steak. On occasion we would be treated to the entertainment of Nat King Cole, Roy Orbison, or other famous singers at the La Fiesta restaurant.

On one visit, some of my Army buddies and I were having a few drinks. They were all smoking and having a good time when one of the guys leaned over and asked me something like "Do you want a drag?"

Since I did not smoke, I said, "No, thanks."

Then he said, "This is not a Camel; 'it's Maryjane.'"

Once again, my naivety stuck out when I asked, "What's that?"

He burst out laughing. That was my first and next-to-last experience around marijuana.

After completion of the training at Fort Bliss, I wound up at Nike Ajax Fire Control Site 73 in the Los Angeles, California, area on Manchester Boulevard. Our radars were located on a small hill a couple of miles from the missile launchers. They were located at the base of the LAX Airport within a couple of blocks of the beach at Playa Del Rey, or the Beach of the King. What a perfect name for this beach! It was pristine and a favorite hangout when we were off duty.

After enduring the barracks for several months, five of us decided to try to rent an apartment. It took several visits to several real estate offices before we found an agent who would help us. Finally, one apartment owner agreed to interview *all* of us; but we had to be together for the interview. Surprisingly, it was a short interview. He rented us the master suite of the building with one stipulation: He could and would inspect our area anytime he wished. We were an interesting bunch, the buddies from Tucson, Arizona, myself, and two other flatlanders from New Mexico.

The landlord came by for the first couple of Saturday mornings to see how things were going; and when he found the apartment all "spit" shined, he even paid us a compliment. It was then we learned that his daughter lived in the apartment above us; and she had told him we were "okay," knew the rules, and followed them. He never dropped by to inspect after that day.

I became friends with the landlord's daughter; and on some of my days off, we would spend time driving Highway 101 along the coast and visiting different beaches. On one weekend we were going to camp out on the beach, but the wind was howling, so we just wrapped up in our beach towels and talked most of the night. Early the next morning, we finished the snacks we had and enjoyed the ocean waves and sounds as it crashed over the rocks. By midafternoon we were tired and headed back to the apartment. As we headed home along Highway 101, it was very warm; and she fell asleep. Unfortunately, I also dozed off. The last thing I remember is standing on the beach, hearing sirens, and seeing police cars up on the highway. At one point I realized that it was my car in that wreck. When I reached the scene, the EMTs were working on an elderly lady who had been driving the other car. When I told the cops I was driving the other car, they immediately whisked me away to do some testing (you know, blood alcohol). When I told them we had been on the beach all night and were just going home when I apparently fell asleep, they used a few choice words, gave me a ticket for reckless driving, and released me. I guess falling asleep at the wheel could be considered the same as "not following the rules."

The elderly lady in the small Volvo station wagon was severely injured and was taken to the local hospital where she remained for several weeks. Over the next few weeks, I went by to check on her to make sure she was going to recover. Her family was not too excited to see me. As it turned out, it was a good thing I had made the effort to see her.

When I stood before the judge to find out what was going to happen to me, his first question was whether or not I had been to see her. I gladly responded in the affirmative that I had seen her and she was to be released the next Monday. His response was "At least you did something right."

After a severe tongue-lashing (which I deserved), he suggested a few rules which I should be following and to which I humbly agreed. Shortly thereafter, I am sure I exhaled a large gush of breath when he announced the fine to be imposed because it was much lower than I had anticipated. At that, he immediately fined me and dismissed me.

While I had been drinking the night before the accident, I was not "under the influence" at the time of the accident. However, it was that accident which gave me a wake-up call.

During the next several months, I began to sense a need to grow up and get on with my life. Common sense told me that it was time to return to college and actually be a student. I applied and was accepted to a small college in western New Mexico. In preparation for college expenses, I began saving every penny. Just before my discharge, I even canceled my car insurance. Later on, this proved to be a less-than-smart move since the rules (and common sense) say you need to have car insurance. I guess I still had not learned that "following the rules" all of the time made sense.

The World's Fair was going on in Seattle when I was discharged. It was a sight I was sure I would never have a second chance to see. So, the day after my discharge, I headed up the coast to Seattle. It was a great experience. However, the trip back to New Mexico did give me another of life's lessons about following the rules.

My June 11, 1962, trip through Arizona led me through the Grand Canyon. My goodness! For a boy from the sand hills of New Mexico, this big hole in the ground was a marvelous sight to see. It was so magnificent that I could not take my eyes off that great big gully. And that distraction from driving put me right into the rear end of the Oldsmobile in front of me. The road was under construction, so I was fortunately cruising along at fifteen to twenty miles per hour. The impact pushed that 1960 Oldsmobile onto the rear of a brand-new Pontiac. This occurred in the middle of the Grand Canyon National Park—no police and no park service employees, just me and the two other drivers and a road crew who wanted us to move on.

Because I had already canceled my car insurance, the only thing I could think to do was to tell these men I would follow them into Flagstaff, Arizona, to the nearest body shop. I told both men once we could get estimates of the cost to repair their cars, I would pay them in cash. Thank goodness no one in either vehicle was injured. The Pontiac repair (a scratch on the brand-new sparkling bright chrome bumper) was estimated at twelve dollars. What a relief! The older gentleman driving the Pontiac was extremely mad and rude even though I had instantly agreed to pay for the damage. I could not believe that little scratch would draw such an unpleasant response.

Because I had pushed the Olds into the Pontiac, the Olds had sustained front and rear damage. The estimate for repairs came to 278.46 dollars. The family in the older model Olds was from Toledo, Ohio, and they had five kids. The gentleman was very cordial, even though I had disrupted their vacation. He wanted to know where I was from and what my plans were. After I had paid him the estimated cost, we exchanged addresses; and I headed out of Flagstaff for Portales, New Mexico, an unintended destination.

Now that the cash was extracted from the old wallet, my plans had to change. I could no longer afford to attend the little college in western New Mexico. So back to my parents' abode I headed. When I finally got settled back home, I wrote the owner of the Olds to again apologize for ruining his family's vacation and thanked him for his kindness and for helping me calm down the driver of the Pontiac.

By returning home and living with my parents (with my tail between my legs), I could still attempt to reenroll at ENMU. This change of plans meant that I had to "appeal" to the dean of students for readmission. If the dean of students would allow me to reenroll, I knew my educational pursuit would be much different this time around. My attitude now was to get a job to pay for tuition and focus only on completing my degree, graduating, and getting on with my life. I dedicated myself to work and study—no dates, no parties, and no fun time, just work and study. The dean of students, after what seemed like a long grueling interview, was gracious and allowed me to enroll in summer school, on probation, with the admonition that if I did well in my summer classes, he would lift my probation.

I had to quickly get a job. That was not a problem. I had a friend whose dad owned Worley Mills Grain Elevator Company. The day I applied for a job, his dad hired me. I thought I would be working in town at the elevator. But, surprise, surprise, my job was to work from 4:00 a.m. to 6:00 a.m. and 4:00 p.m. to 7:00 p.m. five days a week at Worley's hog farm feeding the brood sows and taking care of the piglets. All I had to do was to report to their hog farm at 4:00 a.m. the next morning to begin "slopping the pigs." Then I could work "normal" hours on the weekend.

Not only did I get one job but I got two. My second job was working for C & S Oil Company on the weekends. On Saturdays and Sundays before and after feeding the hogs, I worked from 7:30 a.m. to 7:30 p.m. at the Shamrock gas station located on the Lovington highway. Now my plan was complete. I had a way to pay for my tuition and was committed to completing my degree as soon as possible. Dealing with the pigs could have been humiliating; but after all of my previous screwups, humility came easy; and working with the hogs seemed appropriate even to me. During that time I was also reminded of the prodigal son in Luke 15:11–24.

I held true to my commitment to myself during the summer and made the dean's honor roll. My commitment to no dates and no parties and to just work and study paid off. My academic suspension was lifted, and the fall semester began very smoothly. Work and study were still my routine. As soon as I finished with slopping the hogs, I had to rush home, shower and shave, and hurry to my 8:00 a.m. class. Because of occasional problems on the hog farm, sometimes I ran a little late. On most mornings the only empty seats in the classroom when I arrived were usually on the front row. Due to my limited study time, I generally hustled off after class to the library to study. Sometimes it was beneficial to join a study group. On one occasion a study group member invited me to attend a social mixer at what was referred to as Taylor's Grove (now Oasis State Park), a quiet, secluded, wooded area in the sand dunes a few miles out of town. Attending this mixer turned out to be the second luckiest day of my life.

The university was located in a dry (no alcohol sales) county; so if anyone wished to have any alcoholic beverages at a party, it was necessary to drive eighteen miles to Clovis, New Mexico, in Curry County. Because I was twenty-three, someone in the group asked if I would go to Clovis to purchase some beer for a private party they were going to have after the mixer. I agreed to go and deliver the beer to the mixer, but I told them I would not be joining them. When I arrived at the sandhill party, the group was roasting wieners over a bonfire. When I looked across that bonfire, I gazed into the eyes of the most beautiful blonde I had ever seen or I could even imagine. She was wearing a gold sweatshirt with *Seattle World's Fair* emblazoned on the front. What a great way to start a conversation! "Oh, hi, there. I have just returned from there myself. How did you like it?" We talked for a very long time that evening. When I finally could drag myself away from her, I told my longtime friend David, my hooky-playing friend from first grade, that I was going to marry her. David said something like "Yeah, right, you floppy-eared dude. She won't even remember you after tonight." He was wrong! This *was* indeed the second luckiest day of my life!

Several weeks later I learned that she was in my 8 a.m. class. But she sat in the rear of the room, and that was why I had never seen her in class. Talk about being in too big of a hurry! The next time I saw her, I asked her to go out for a hotdog at Luke's Drive In. From that night on we dated every night *except for the homecoming dance.* (Now when I say dated, I mean that we got together and studied in the library or at the dinner table of my parents' home.) She already had been asked and accepted a date for another homecoming event. I went to the dance without her; but lucky, lucky me, that was the last time either of us had a date with someone else. A few months later, I proposed to her; and her response made me deliriously happy. It was the luckiest day of my life.

I will never forget the day we told my dad that we were going to get married. That Saturday Dad was sitting on the couch in the living room reading the newspaper. When I told him we were going to get married, he did not say "Congratulations" or "Good luck." As a matter of fact, he said nothing to me. He just glanced up, looked at Carolyn, and said, "As long as I am alive, he will never leave you."

I don't know if he ever had that same conversation with my brothers, but all of us remained married until they or their spouses passed away. We were married on July 12, 1963, exactly nine months after meeting at Taylor's Grove. In the summer of 2018, we celebrated our fifty-fifth wedding anniversary.

During our college days we had several classes together. She was not only beautiful; she was bright and always made better grades than I did. One class which turned out to be memorable was business law. We always studied together for the classes we had together and always sat next to each other in those classes. We made the exact same score on the business law midterm exam. When the professor was passing out the papers, he made some comment to the class about how we should not sit next to each other during the next exam because of our identical scores. This made me furious. (My wife would never cheat. Me? Well?)

Anyway, I took great exception to his comments. For this class we had a workbook, and all test questions came from the workbook. And all questions were true or false questions. After giving the situation a little thought, I decided we would fill out the workbook and then only study the *true* questions. So when we took the final exam, if we recognized the question, it had to be true. The final exam had one hundred questions, and we had one hour to complete it. I completed my exam in about fifteen minutes. The professor was very surprised when I turned in my paper. He asked me if I was sure I had completed the entire exam, did I miss a page, or something. I simply said "I don't believe I had time to look at anyone else's answers. Do you?" and left. My wife was about five minutes behind me. I know I did not learn a lot about business law, but I did get some satisfaction in making sure he would know that we did not cheat on his exams. We did however make an A on the exam.

Classes went well for both of us, but finances seemed to always be a problem. I had traded my expensive-to-operate beautiful bright red-and-black 1955 Buick two-door sedan for a Volkswagen bug which had been constructed out of the junkyard. It had a cloth roof, no heater, and fenders of three different colors; but it was cheap to operate. I supported my new wife in "style," so we lived in the married student housing on campus like all of the other working stiffs.

During our third semester together, we were living in the student housing area called Vetville, our first "home." One morning the floor of the bathroom collapsed! The termites had eaten the floor through and through. Our "home" was one of the old military barracks from the Fort Sumner Air Force Base which was closed shortly after WWII ended. The barracks and one airplane hangar had been moved from Fort Sumner, New Mexico, to the campus. The hangar served as our college gym, and the barracks were the married student housing.

Working on the hog farm and pumping gas were not the most financially rewarding jobs, but I was happy to have the work. On a couple of occasions, we were very short on cash. One week we did not even have the money to buy groceries. I was very worried about how I was going to handle the situation as I was too proud and embarrassed to ask anyone for help.

It might seem preposterous to some folks; but, when we needed financial help the most, we received a miracle. In the mail that week, I received a thirty-five-dollar refund from my 1962 telephone deposit from Westminster, California. Talk about manna from heaven. Again, that year we were not sure how we were going to pay for tuition. Once again God intervened and sent us manna from heaven! On August 4, 1962, I received a letter from the family man I had run into during my drive through the Grand Canyon. It contained money orders totaling the difference of the estimate we received from the body shop in Flagstaff, Arizona, and the actual cost of repair when he returned to Toledo, Ohio.

It made me proud and brought me to tears at the same time. The letter said in part:

> We hope the enclosed money orders prove somewhat of a pleasant surprise to you considering the circumstances.
>
> The local Oldsmobile Dealer repaired my car completely to my satisfaction for a total price of $125.25 instead of the $278.46 estimated by the mechanic in Flagstaff. I am returning your postal money orders for $100.00 and $8.74 together with another for $44.17 which represents the balance of the $169.72 I received from you in Flagstaff less the costs of the postal money order and the repairs to my car.

Another paragraph stated:

> Receiving one copy of the Flagstaff estimate returned from New Mexico Western (the college where I had applied) unopened then your letter from Portales indicated to us that you must have missed getting back to college. We certainly hope the return of this $152.91 will help you resume your studies this fall. Your conduct and display of integrity in this matter have been highly commendable, and we want to wish you the best of luck in the future.
>
> Yours truly,
> Donald J. Miller.

Needless to say, we were surprised and elated. I was very impressed by Mr. Miller's concern about my future; and I learned a new lesson about *following the rules*, even if they are not written. Ronald Reagan's definition of character is correct! In our conversation after the wreck, Mr. Miller told me that he was an accountant;

so his meticulous accounting of the costs did not surprise me. But with five kids, he could certainly have kept and used the money; and I never would have known. His actions gave me a new appreciation for people with high moral values, values that urge folks to do the right thing even when no one is looking.

My perspective on finances was much different than a lot of my college classmates. It was never more apparent than when one friend asked me to join a business fraternity. He invited me to come to a fraternity rush party to get acquainted with some of the members. I attended not knowing what to expect. A few days later I asked him what it would cost to join. When he said 150 dollars to join and 150 dollars a month for dues, I almost laughed out loud.

When I told him I could not afford it, he said (and I will never forget his words), "Do what I do and take it out of your allowance."

"Allowance!" I responded. "I don't get an allowance. I am working on a hog farm for thirty-five cents an hour."

Later, my wonderful wife and I did join FBLA, a business fraternity; but it was one we could afford. During that time, I was elected president of FBLA. The fraternity had several professional trips to various cities and businesses. On one occasion we scheduled a trip to Colorado to tour Colorado Fuel and Iron in Pueblo and to visit the US Mint in Denver. For some reason, which I do not recall, our sponsor was not going to be able to chaperone the group. Consequently, the dean of students (my old friend) was not going to allow us to make the trip. Our sponsor then convinced the dean that we (Carolyn and I) were married and responsible, so we should be allowed to be members *and* chaperone the group. Before letting us go, the dean made sure we knew the rules and made us pledge to follow them.

As a side note Dean Shutt became the butt of a prank during one Halloween. Some students found an outdoor toilet and brought it to the front lawn of the administration building. In big bold letters they had named it the "Shutt House." No, I was not involved!

After graduation we moved to Denver, Colorado, where I enrolled in the University of Denver Law School. During the enrollment process, the dean of admissions warned everyone that we needed to devote our full-time efforts to studying for classes. He strongly advised against trying to work and attend law school. My thought was I had to have some income because I had a wife to support. And I had made it okay in my undergraduate program; and, by golly, I thought I could do it here. So I got a job at May D & F Department Store in downtown Denver. As it turned out, the dean was right. I could not work and keep my grades up, so it was time to move on. Now I needed a full-time job to support my family. I landed one at Central Bank and Trust which was located at 15th and Arapahoe Streets in downtown Denver.

Here I learned some more valuable lessons about following the rules. I also learned one funny lesson about how to beat some of the rules. I was given the title of credit adjustor (better known as a bill collector). One of my accounts was a nurse who was a very good customer. She had financed a new 1964 Mustang through the installment loan department. For some reason unknown to me, she fell behind in her payments; so I asked her to come in to discuss her account. When she came in, we had a short chat in which she disclosed to me that she had married a race car driver and they were having some financial difficulties. Because of her prior credit experience, I adjusted her loan payment schedule; and she went on her way. Several months later she again fell behind in her payments, so once again I invited her into the office. She parked in the bank parking lot and came to my office, which was on the third floor.

During that visit, it became apparent that her circumstances had drastically changed and she would no longer be able to make her payments. It was my sad duty to inform her I was repossessing her car and it could not leave the parking lot. When she refused to give me her keys, I signaled one of the other adjustors to go down to the parking lot and remove the coil wire from the distributor in her car to disable it. When he returned, I ended the conversation. As she left the office, several of the adjustors joined me at our third floor window; and we watched her as she exited the building and entered her car. We heard her trying to start the car. When it did not start, she exited the car, opened the hood, surveyed the situation, pulled a spark plug wire loose, used it as a coil wire to the distributor, jumped back into the car, started it, and drove off. The laugh was on me! I had *followed the rules*, but she drove around them. Apparently, her time with her race car driver husband had taught her something about cars.

Just got married! Luckiest day of my life. Leaving the
church to change clothes to go on our honeymoon.

Carolyn and I leaving on our "overnight" honeymoon
to Ruidoso, NM in a borrowed car.

CHAPTER 18

MY FAITH JOURNEY

Many years later, the following scripture became very meaningful to me:

> Start children off on the way they should go, and even when they are old they will not turn from it. (Proverbs 22:6)

Did my Christian journey of faith make me stubborn? My early faith journey did not include my family. Attending church was not a part of my family life. As a matter of fact, I had never attended a regular Sunday church service with my parents. One of my older brothers and his wife did attend one Sunday service with me, but none of my other five siblings ever attended with me. However, two of my brothers were regular attendees during their early family raising years; but for various reasons, they stopped. In retrospect, I can only remember two times that I was in a church with my parents. The first was at the wedding of my oldest brother, Ed, and his bride, Wilma Gregory. The last time was at the wedding of my next oldest brother, Charlie, and his bride, Sunnye Jean Lee.

It wasn't because the four of them did not believe in God; but family situations, squabbles within their congregations, and schedules of family responsibilities all became "reasons" not to become and/or stay active. It was not until after my dad passed away that I discovered why my mom and dad never attended church. I was told that, when my dad was thirteen or fourteen, he attended a cowboy camp revival outside of Trinchera, Colorado. At the end of the service the preacher was passing out Bibles, and my dad accepted one. The next afternoon the preacher came to the cow camp where my dad was working and told him he should not have taken the Bible because he did not pay for it. Apparently, my dad believed he was being accused of stealing. Dad never went near any preacher after that.

The earliest memory I have of my personal faith journey is during my third grade year. We were living on Lime Street in Portales, New Mexico, approximately two miles from the Presbyterian church. I cannot give an explanation as to why I was drawn to church, but on Sundays I would walk to church by myself. My parents did not encourage or discourage me from going. My mom did make sure that I was wearing clean clothes. That little church was where I met preacher Rev. Homer Ackers. He was a wonderful, friendly, jolly kind of fellow who always made me feel welcome.

When we moved from Lime Street to State Street, it was too far for me to walk to the Presbyterian church; so I stopped attending any church. I returned to church when we moved to the house on the Lovington highway. It was a great surprise that my first grade friend David lived just two blocks away. His folks would pick me up every Sunday and take me to the Methodist church with them. Even after they moved a couple of miles out of town, they continued to pick me up every Sunday morning. I wonder what Mr. Hart would have said if he had known that on some Sundays David would sneak into his mom's purse and take her car keys so we could take their car after Sunday school and drive around instead of attending church and listening to the sermon. The Harts were a "God send" to me and exemplified what Jesus commanded all Christians to do when he issued his great commission (Matthew 28:16–20).

Orville Smith lived across the street from David, and the three of us were good buddies. During cotton-picking time, Mr. Smith would take me with them to pick cotton. I remember those long heavy cotton sacks were hard to drag behind you as you stripped the cotton stalks and shoved the cotton into them. When we were about thirteen, Orville was killed in a pickup accident in Colorado. His funeral was the first funeral I remember attending. David and I were pallbearers.

Some of my classmates in junior high attended the Baptist church which was located one block away from the Methodist church. On Sunday afternoons the Baptists had a youth program called something like Royal Ambassadors. I liked some of those Baptist girls; and since they said anyone could come, I went. My participation with these fine young ladies ended abruptly one Sunday morning when I attended Sunday school with them. During the lesson the teacher asked anyone who was a Christian to stand up. *Well*, I knew all of these kids pretty well and knew an awful lot about them; so, when they stood up, I laughed. Apparently, laughing was inappropriate. At least that was what I was told. So I never returned to the Baptist church. My goodness, they had no sense of humor.

Thanks to the Harts, I did however return to the Methodist church where I attended confirmation classes with my buddy David. After graduating from confirmation class, David and I were baptized. We chose to be immersed. Because the Methodist church did not have a baptistery, we were baptized in the First Baptist Church on a Sunday afternoon. The ladies at the Methodist church were always very friendly to me on Sundays, and I really liked being there. They didn't seem to mind that my parents were not involved.

Not every event in my faith journey was a positive one! That summer I heard about a back-to-school party being held at the local country club for junior high students. The country club was about two miles outside of town. I wanted to go, so I walked to the clubhouse. When I got to the entrance, one of the ladies I had met at church asked me if I had received an invitation. I didn't know one needed an invitation! When I said no, she asked me to wait while she checked with someone else. When she returned, she said I would be welcome if I would go home and change into a coat and tie and then return. There was that "following the rules" thing again. Well, sports fans, I did not own a dress coat or a tie. The same nice folks who had welcomed me at church without a coat or tie now turned me away from that party. I was embarrassed and furious. I no longer had any desire to go to church with "those" people. It now seemed very odd to me that I would leave the church so soon after being baptized, but forgiveness was not part of my understanding at that time.

I told myself that I would never be embarrassed again because I did not have a coat and tie. I worked at every little job I could get, picking cotton (actually pulling bowls), crating sweet potatoes for twenty-five cents a crate, picking green beans and being paid by the bushel basket, and weeding fields and getting paid by the hour. Once I had saved enough cash, I bought me a white sports coat, a black pair of pants, a belt woven with pink and charcoal material, and a pink and charcoal tie. Boy, was I proud! I attended every dance that came along just like I was somebody.

This attitude was what led me to get acquainted with the local sheriff. I was so mad at these church folks that I took advantage of some of them by prowling their streets and alleys looking for easy-to-sell items as a way to get a few easy bucks in pursuit of a coat and tie. One day a friend needed some hay to feed his horse. So a few buddies and I told him we would help him out and get him some hay. We relieved another friend's dad of some hay. This was my first experience with the local law enforcement folks. I was certainly embarrassed when the sheriff pulled us out of class the day they decided we were involved. It did lead me and my dad to once again have a trip to the office of an authority figure—this time to the juvenile judge's courtroom. When the judge asked me why I had taken the hay, I told him I did not have an answer. My dad grabbed me by my collar (that was becoming a regular routine) and gave me a look I never wanted to see again. The judge quickly spoke to my dad and told him he was releasing me into his custody and that he had better never see me again. I assured him he would not. This promise seemed to be the right thing to say at the time. However, I was not sure I would make it home alive.

Lucky for me I was still involved in the Boy Scouts. During grade school and junior high, I was active in the Scouts. I loved the Scouts. We went camping and attended camporees (a weekend where several troops camped out together and competed in various scouting skills and worked on merit badges). At our weekly meetings, we played all kinds of games. Eventually I earned my Life badge and was tapped out for the Order of the Arrow at Camp We-Hen-Ah-Pay, our conference summer camp. Memorizing the Scout Oath and Scout Promise was one of the first tasks I accomplished; and I have never forgotten them or what they stand for, even though I did not always follow them. At this time in my life, I guess this was my only contact with any kind of faith commitment because each week I would pledge to keep myself morally straight.

I only continued in the Scouts because of my older brother Charlie who came home after he was discharged from the Army. His mission was to complete his prelaw classes at ENMU, but he also took time to be the scoutmaster of my scout troop. As I look back on those days, I know I was blessed because he was the main reason I remained in scouting.

I learned a lot about leadership and everyday skills, which I still use today. The need to follow the rules was drilled into us as a safety issue. Several incidents drove home the value of rules. It seems odd now that I can still remember some of those skills. They even became valuable in my career—things like "getting and giving information," "knowing and using the resources of the group," and "setting the example." Life was good, but I decided that girls and earning some spending money were more important if I wanted to date the girls and be allowed to go to those fancy dances. Jobs and chasing girls eventually won out, so I no longer had time for the Scouts.

When we moved to Avenue D, it proved to be a blessing for me. Here was where my friend Jere Beasley's grandmother, Granny Ryan, mentored me and inspired me in many ways. I was not a very good student in high school; but, with Granny Ryan's encouragement, my scholastic prowess improved. I guess Jere was also a good influence on me.

Granny became a very good friend and confidant. To me she was a perfect example of what a Christian is supposed to be. Granny was a very frail, elderly lady who loved the Lord. Every Sunday morning, rain or shine, snow or wind, you could see her walking to the Nazarene church. She knew that my family did not attend any church and that, on occasion, I had been going to church off and on by myself since I was in the third grade. She was also aware that the Harts picked me up on most Sunday mornings.

One evening we were sitting on her front porch in her swing when she engaged me in a conversation about "where I was heading." She was aware that I had stopped attending church regularly, and she was concerned about my relationship with the Lord. It was a long conversation which I will always remember. She asked me to consider the following: "If you live all of your life believing in God and when you die there is no God, you have lost nothing. But you will have lived among the finest people in the world. Your friends will be many, and all of your days will be filled with joy." However, she said, "If when you die there is a God, as I believe there is, and you die as a nonbeliever, you will have lost eternal life and the glory of God. Think about it." I did, and I have never forgotten that conversation as it made an everlasting impression on me. However, it took many years before I really understood what she was trying to tell me.

Another lady helped me understand what Granny Ryan was talking about. She reintroduced me to the church. She is my wonderful Christian wife who has attended church all of her life. Every Sunday after we got married, she would invite me to attend worship services with her. I graciously (at least, I hope I was gracious) declined. Sundays were my days to stay home and worship the Denver Broncos on television. She never gave up. My loving wife was very patient, consistent, and persistent as she lovingly invited to me to church every Sunday. After our kids were born, I began to reconsider my faith responsibilities to my children. First, I became what I refer to as a C and E Christian. That was when I went to church on Christmas and Easter. After her consistent loving invites, I finally succumbed and began attending regularly. Eventually, we became the youth group sponsors; and later I began helping with the Boy Scout troop, which the church sponsored. I was honored to be an assistant scoutmaster for the Conquistador Council troop that went to the 1982 National Jamboree at Fort A.P. Hill, Virginia. I continued my involvement in scouting for over twenty-five years.

During my senior year in high school, several of my friends and I joined the National Guard. Originally, we joined to make a few bucks. Later we discovered we could check out rifles and ammunition, ostensibly for target practice. Actually we would go rabbit hunting. During one summer camp, Jere, David, my brother Tom, and I volunteered to go early and be part of the advanced-unit convoy to drive ten or twelve vehicles to Fort Sill, Oklahoma. This gave us the opportunity to earn some extra pay for this two-day trip. We had two drivers per vehicle. As it turned out we had a Jere and a Jerry in our detachment. One Jere was my Anglo neighbor, and the other Jerry was an African American guardsman from Clovis, New Mexico. During the trip we were on our own for meals (rations were issued, but yuck). During lunch one day we stopped at a little café in a small town in Texas for lunch. When we were filing in and getting settled at tables, a waitress went over to the table where Jerry was sitting. In a voice loud enough for all of us to hear, she told Jerry, "You cannot eat in the dining room. You will have to go in the back." Almost instantly everyone jumped to their feet and as we exited the café, we told her if Jerry had to eat in the back, we would all eat elsewhere. From there we went to a small grocery store, bought lunch meat and bread for sandwiches, and went to the little city park and had lunch. I had heard about racism, but this was my first exposure to blatant racism. I believe we were all reminded we should be treating others as we wanted to be treated.

My interests in sports continued, but at a different level and for different reasons. One of my colleagues in Portales was the head track coach at ENMU. In college he was the roommate of Gale Sayers. He invited Gale to be the guest speaker at a fund-raiser for the track team. Soon after that speech, I purchased his book entitled *I Am Third*. The point of the book for him was he came after God and his family, as he was third in his priorities. For me it was a very inspirational book which I used years later to encourage the boys in my scout troop. At this point in my life, I finally understood the verse "Start children off on the way they should go, and even when they are old they will not turn from it" (Proverbs 22:6). I urged them to emulate Gale in sports and life.

I prayed that my own children would not do what I had done in my early years. My prayers were answered! They were never in any trouble and are a blessing to us.

For many years I believed Bible studies were for kids and they were to be pursued on Sundays during Sunday school classes. During these early years of our marriage, we moved from Portales, New Mexico; to Denver, Colorado; to Houston, Texas; back to Portales; and on to El Paso, Texas, and finally retired in the mountains of southern New Mexico. Members of each church I attended helped me grow in my faith. As my faith grew over the years, I eventually joined my wife in teaching Sunday school classes. All the time we lived in El Paso, we attended Western Hills United Methodist Church and attended Sunday school. What a blessing this was for me!

On numerous occasions in El Paso, I was invited to attend various evening Bible study classes. My excuses were always I just didn't have the time. Finally, a good friend of mine invited me to attend a short course that would meet one night a week for only three weeks. Because he was teaching the class, I said "yes." That short class led me to a six-week class which led to me participate in seven continuous years of one-night-a-week Bible studies. The friends I made there have grown into lifelong friends. We still get together for reunions even though most of us have moved from El Paso and are scattered throughout the country. My faith deepened as I attended Bible studies and adult Sunday school classes.

In 1993 one of my friends, Les Penner, invited me to attend a personal Christian growth weekend called the Walk to Emmaus. I would not say he was a pest, but he sure was persistent. For a couple of years, my old excuses for not attending worked. Then one Sunday he was in a conversation with me and two of my friends. Previously, he had invited each of us to attend Emmaus. On this Sunday Dick said he would go if I would go. He was sure I was not going. My response was I would go if Rush would go because I knew that he wouldn't. Boy, was I surprised when Rush said yes. Right then Dick and I knew that we were all hooked. Hooked is the wrong word. That weekend proved to be one of the very best spiritual experiences of my life. The Emmaus weekend is based on Luke, chapter 24:13–31. Emmaus activities continue to be a major part of my life.

That Emmaus weekend forced me to reflect on who I was, whose I was, and why I was still alive. Ephesians 4:22–24 says:

> So get rid of your old self, which made you live as you used to—the old self which was being destroyed by its deceitful desires. Your hearts and minds must be made completely new. (Good News for Modern Man, 1966)

The real question to me was: "Why am I still alive? What should my purpose in life be?" That may seem a little overdramatic, but on reflection I believe that I survived three near-death experiences for a reason. But what was it?

The first of these three experiences was on that Christmas Eve in 1950 when I jumped out of the car. Recently during a family reunion, my sister-in-law Wilma was recounting her experiences after joining the Durrett family. One of those experiences was seeing me during that Christmas weekend. She told me that she almost vomited when she saw me that day because I was one large scab. She said I looked like raw meat. My memory of that Christmas day is a little different. I can still remember my brother Jerry coming into the bedroom on Christmas morning teasing me and showing me the jigsaw "we" had received as our Christmas gift. We still were not in the money, but Dad had gotten us a store-bought gift—a real jigsaw! He had also bought each of us a small pocket knife, which I treasured until I lost it years later. I could not even move my hands to touch the jigsaw or open my knife. I still believe Jerry was teasing me to watch me squirm.

My second near-death experience was during a drunken stupor on the way to Taylor's Grove. I had been drinking all day long, and as my friend Bob Simpson drove out the Cannon Air Force Base Highway toward Taylor's Grove, I crawled out of the car window and onto the roof of the car. Reason? No, there was no reason other than stupidity. Just after Bob pulled off of the highway onto the dirt road, he slammed on his brakes. He thought it would be funny to watch me fly off the roof. It worked. This sudden stopping threw me off the roof onto the hood and down in front of the sliding car. I am extremely thankful for two issues: One was that the station wagon he was driving did not have an ornament in the center of the hood. If it had had one, it would have ripped my belly wide open. The second was when Bob stopped the car just inches from my limp, unconscious body. I was under the bumper next to the tire. It was another undeserved miracle, a God thing! There were no broken bones, just a shirt ripped to shreds and a skinned shoulder. I had been wearing a shirt my mother had made me from a Golden West flour sack. I did not know how to explain the torn-up shirt to my mom. I was sure she would not believe a story about falling off of a car roof, so that was what I told her.

Earlier I related my third experience of surviving a head-on collision on Highway 101 during my time in California. I was not injured, and my passenger was not injured, but the lady driving the Volvo station wagon was severely injured. I believe that God must have been watching over me because we all survived.

After my Emmaus weekend in May of 1993, I began to reflect on those past experiences and why I was still alive. I began to believe then and I still believe now that God must have had a purpose for me, or I would be dead. I am still attempting to determine what my purpose on earth is and then to do His will. My faith journey continues.

Could my purpose be participating in Kairos Prison Ministry? One of my Emmaus friends invited me to attend the closing event of a Kairos weekend at the New Mexico state prison in Santa Fe, New Mexico. During the last event of the weekend, Gordon, a prisoner, asked to speak. He made the following statement as tears were streaming down his cheeks and he struggled to speak. His comments went like this:

> The last time I was in church, I was attending a Bible study class. The only thing this church seemed to talk about was money—give

more, sacrifice more. I became so discouraged that I stood up, tore up my Bible and my study materials, threw them in the waste basket, and stormed out.

He said he had always been told about God's love but had never experienced it. He continued:

I only came to this weekend because of the food I heard you were bringing.

Then he said:

Because of the crimes I have committed, I will never leave the prison system. But this weekend I have experienced what Christian love is all about; and I am at peace with myself, with the legal system, and with the punishment I deserve. You volunteered to come inside; you did not judge me; you just shared your Christian love.

Gordon's witness convinced me that I should be an active part of sharing Christ's love with the incarcerated. I have been blessed beyond my wildest imagination during my last twenty-four years by participating in Kairos. During these years I might have spent more daytime hours behind prison bars than many prisoners because of the Kairos model. Team members are inside the prison from Thursday afternoon through Sunday afternoon (no, we do not spend the nights, just an average of eight to ten hours each day) for around forty hours each Kairos weekend. In addition, some members of the team return to that prison one Saturday each month. In prisons which allow the program, it is normal to have two Kairos weekends per year. For several years I was able to join a team three or four times per year, serving in a federal institution and three New Mexico state prisons.

I can only describe a Kairos weekend as an event where God performs miracles and changes lives and allows the Kairos volunteers to watch. Kairos is based on Matthew 25:36, "I was in prison and you visited me."

These faith-building experiences helped me to deal with my own turbulent encounters with Superintendent Vargas, the school board members, and the SBEC staff as they all took what I believed to be illegal and inappropriate actions which created unforeseen setbacks for me.

I will forever be thankful to Rev. Steve McElroy. He was my pastor at Western Hills United Methodist Church in El Paso during my ordeal. I loved his sermons and his general demeanor. To me he was always upbeat and looking on the bright side of life. Because I did not want to jeopardize my lawsuit, I did not talk about my situation as a general rule. If someone had read about it in the newspaper or heard about it and asked, I would respond as succinctly as possible. It was my problem, and I was going to handle it. I did not want others involved, especially the employees who worked for me because they might also be targeted for retaliation. I believed that I did not need any help other than my attorneys. Boy, was I wrong! I needed my spiritual supporters in my church, my Emmaus reunion group, and my Kairos reunion groups praying for me. "The Lord protects the unwary; when I was brought low, he saved me" (Psalm 116:6).

One afternoon when I was on my pity potty, I dropped by Pastor Steve's office, crying in my beer about the last SBEC ruling which could be a real setback if it was not reversed. He was his ole jolly, good-natured self. When I stepped into his office, he took one look at me and said something like "What rock did you just crawl out from under? You look like hell." Then he started laughing and motioning for me to sit down and asking me what was going on.

Once I composed myself and filled him in on what had happened and the potential downside of the last SBEC ruling, he made my day! When I asked why I could feel so bad about doing what I believed to be the right thing, he said, "My friend, I have known you for several years now; and I know whatever happens, you and the school district will be better off for it." Then all of a sudden, he said, "I read the newspaper; you are my hero." Now I have been called a lot of things before in my lifetime, but never a hero.

After the depositions were over, other than Pastor Steve, I only shared my thoughts with my wife and the Emmaus reunion group or the monthly Kairos reunion with the prisoners. My Emmaus group met every Saturday morning at 6:00 a.m. at the church. This was my safe zone where I could talk about it and know that it would not be discussed elsewhere. They were my support group for which I will forever be thankful.

CHAPTER 19

NOTHING BUT THE TRUTH: FILLING IN THE BLANKS

Occasionally, I reflected on my current conflict with Vargas and pondered my prior experiences. I reminded myself that my resolve to *follow the rules* had been tested before.

As I look back on the legal process, I am still amazed at the length of efforts made and expense incurred by the board to fire me for filing a legal whistle-blower complaint. As I outline the legal wrangling as it transpired in the discovery process, please remember that *the original complaint was originated by the parents of several students*. I simply formalized it on their behalf and filed it with the appropriate state agency. The parents' complaints are briefly summarized as follows:

1. A teacher violated his ethical oath by offering his students (their children) extra credit on their midterm grades for distributing political flyers for two candidates for positions in the local school board.

2. This extra credit was for approximately two hours of effort distributing campaign flyers. (Coincidentally, one of the candidates receiving this benefit was a sitting member on the school board seeking reelection.)

Once the principal interviewed the teacher and reviewed the lesson plans, he stated that the teacher:

1. Did not include the task in his lesson plans as required
2. Did not ask the students to submit any critique of the election process or any academic evaluation of the candidate's position on any topic being discussed in the election
3. Submitted a written statement in which he admitted the facts as described by the students and alleged by the parents

It was during this time frame that the legal maneuvering intensified. Now the district was trying every defense they or their attorneys could dream up, reminding me that some smart person once said, "The wheels of justice grind slowly." I can only add that while the wheels of justice grinds slowly the costs of justice run much faster because of the convoluted legal processes of the court system. A high school friend, Ronnie Cox, sings a song whose lyrics described how I was feeling. He says, "It is a dog-eat-dog world out there, and it seems like I am wearing milk bone underwear."

After I was fired for insubordination, I filed my lawsuit in federal court. I was now fighting the district through the SBEC and in the United States District Court for the Western District of Texas, El Paso Division. It was also enlightening to watch Vargas and the board members dodge questions and lose their memories when responding to specific questions.

Throughout the early proceedings, Mr. Luther Jones was the lead defense attorney defending Vargas, the board, and the teacher accused of violating the code of ethics. As my lawsuit progressed, the board enlisted the services of three separate law firms. Remember my allegations were only three violations of my rights, including the Texas Whistle-Blower Act and my constitutional rights granted under the First and Fourteenth Amendments. I guess they needed one law firm for each allegation.

Now that the district had responded alleging several defenses, my attorneys began the discovery process by taking the depositions to fill in the blanks.

Dr. Vargas was deposed beginning "Tuesday, January 18, 2000, at 2:03 p.m., and Wednesday, January 19, 2000, at 7:04 a.m."

The first defense articulated by Dr. Vargas in his deposition was that I had filed the complaint on behalf of the district:

> Q: Did you terminate Dr. Durrett for a failure of the district review committee…or for other reasons relating to this insubordination or the failure to withdraw the complaint?
>
> A: But the point is, is that when he was recommended for termination, it was because of his refusal to follow a directive to withdraw a complaint *filed by the district* against an employee during…as a result of an investigation that was incomplete and still in process. (Emphasis added) (Vargas, page 58)

The operative words in his answer are "filed by the district" because his contention was that my complaint was filed on behalf of the district and not personally by me. His assertion was that my failure to follow his directive and withdraw the complaint was insubordination. If the judge agreed I had filed the complaint on behalf of the district, then my firing was legal; and I would be out of luck with a lot of attorney's fees.

Mr. Jones raised this defense, and others, in many different ways in court filings and in his pleadings to the SBEC, when requesting them to withdraw my complaint.

Another attempt to obfuscate the issues by Vargas was to allege that:

> Dr. Durrett took disciplinary action against the employee when he filed the complaint against the SBEC without my knowledge or approval or review, did not keep the board or myself apprised, and told me after the fact. (Vargas, page 69)

My position that the filing of a complaint was not taking disciplinary action was confirmed by Ms. Strashun:

> Q: With respect to the complaint filed with the SBEC against (the teacher) by Dr. Durrett, did Dr. Durrett request any specific sanction be taken against or imposed upon (the teacher)?
>
> A: No. (Strashun, question 24)

In addition, Vargas's statement had four separate allegations, three of which were false because, in accordance with SBEC policies, Dr. Vargas was mailed a certified copy of the complaint on July 3, 1999, return receipt request #Z184 282 606. Also, SBEC regulations do not require anyone's approval or that a filing be reported to anyone including him or the board for purposes of review before filing a complaint. The fourth was indeed true! He was told after the fact because, in accordance with SBEC regulations, he received a copy of the complaint through the US Postal Service, via certified mail.

Throughout the process, Vargas continued to insist that I had not filed the complaint as an individual. His contention was that the complaint was a district complaint, filed by me. Questions and answers regarding this issue begin on page 107 of his deposition:

> Q: Do you know whether or not the Ysleta Independent School District is named as a complainant or Dr. Durrett?
>
> A: I believe the document states Dr. Durrett as having placed his name on the form as the person making the complaint filling out the form. But it is a district complaint based on confidential personnel records that only he would have access to, filed on district stationery using district resources, district time. He would not have had that information available to him as a private citizen, not with-

out a release of records from (the teacher) and the students giving him access to confidential records. That is a district complaint that he filed in his position as associate superintendent.

Q: Did you tell Dr. Durrett that this is a district complaint to the SBEC?

A: It was… I don't know if I used those specific terms. But I said it was inappropriate for him to file a complaint at this point since the investigation was incomplete…(Vargas, pages 107–108)

When questioned regarding whether or not he needed to approve complaints filed against him with the SBEC, he responded in the following Q and A. His responses begin on page 109 of his deposition:

Q: Did Dr. Durrett have…did he require your permission to file the complaint against you with the SBEC?

A: I don't know if he…he did not have…he did not ask me about it. He filed it.

Q: Did he require your permission or authority to file a complaint against you?

A: I don't believe he did.

Q: Why not?

A: Well, if he wants to file…whether it's appropriate or not is another question. Whether he can file one? He filed one. I don't know. As we stated earlier, I'm not familiar with SBEC rules, so I don't know what the guidelines are of the specifics of who can file, under what grounds and which ones are…(Vargas, pages 109–110)

Q: Can you explain to me why you believe that he had…that it was up to him whether he can file a complaint against you, but it was not up to him whether he can file a complaint against (the teacher)?

A: He didn't file a complaint against (the teacher) as an individual. He filed it as a school district employee, and that was without my authority or without my approval and without my knowledge. He kept it from me.

Q: In what capacity did Dr. Durrett file the complaint against you, as a school district employee?

A: I have not reviewed it in enough detail or talked to Dr. Durrett or Mr. Luther Jones about it enough to be able to tell you what the status is or the conditions or whether it's a valid filing. And I don't know the SBEC rules.

Q: Did you direct the SBEC to withdraw the complaint that Dr. Durrett had made against (the teacher)?

A: I sent them a letter requesting that it be withdrawn. (Vargas, page 110)

This line of defense continued even though Vargas's letter to the SBEC requesting them to withdraw the complaint indicated otherwise:

Q: Let me provide you Exhibit 17, which is an August 18, 1999, letter to Jackie Strashun. Is that a letter that you wrote?

A: This was drafted, yes, by myself and with review by Mr. Jones.

Q: And Luther Jones is copied on this?

A: Yes.

Q: As the district legal counsel. Is that correct?

A: Yes.

Q: Now, as of August 18, were you aware that Luther Jones was also representing (the teacher) in front of the SBEC?

A: I don't recall if I knew that or not.

Q: You state in paragraph 2 that, I did request Dr. Durrett to withdraw his complaint. Do you see that?

A: Yes.

Q: Now you refer to the complaint as "his complaint." Is that indicative of what you believed on August 18 that it was Dr. Durrett's complaint and not the Ysleta Independent School District complaint?

A: No. The Ysleta Independent School District complaint that he filed in his role as associate superintendent. (Vargas, page 111)

The operative word in this question is "his," meaning me, ole Bob, a.k.a. Dr. Durrett:

The attempt to have my complaint seen as a district complaint continued:

Q: With all due respect, I don't see that language in that letter. I see the term "his complaint." And your testimony now is "his complaint" refers to the Ysleta Independent School District complaint?

A: Yes. He filled out the form using school district confidential information, resources, and under his position as associate superintendent. (Vargas, page 112)

Further questioning revealed what seemed to me to be very peculiar logic of Vargas regarding whether I filed the complaint or it was a district complaint (Vargas, pages 114–115):

> Q: Now, I'll represent to you that you and I have learned that the SBEC believes that the attorney for (the teacher) is Luther Jones. Do you understand that?
>
> A: Okay.
>
> Q: And you stated that Luther Jones conferred with you in the drafting of this letter. Is that correct?
>
> A: That's correct.
>
> Q: So is it the case that you are asking on behalf of the Ysleta Independent School District that a complaint be suspended or withdrawn as to one of Mr. Jones' clients, who is an employee of the district?
>
> A: No. When this letter was written, it was simply to communicate that...to the office of investigations and enforcement that I had requested Dr. Durrett withdraw his complaint on behalf of the district to the SBEC until the investigation was complete.

Questioning continued on page 115:

> Q: I don't ever see the terms "Dr. Durrett's complaint on behalf of the district" showing up in any memorandum or letter. Can you point to any letter that you authored where you refer to the complaint as Dr. Durrett's complaint on behalf of the district?
>
> A: I don't recall if I can at this point.

Vargas was questioned several more times regarding whether or not he ever memorialized, in writing, his belief that the (teacher) complaint was filed on behalf of the district. The last reference I will refer to now came in this Q and A on page 119 of his deposition:

> Q: In exhibit 19, you refer to the complaint filed by Dr. Durrett against (the teacher). Do you see that?
>
> A: Mm-hm.
>
> Q: And again, in this memorandum you do not state that it is a complaint filed by Dr. Durrett on behalf of the Ysleta Independent School District, do you?
>
> A: I do state to withdraw a complaint filed by you, Dr. Durrett.
>
> Q: But you don't indicate that it's a district complaint in any written memorandum or letter at about this time, do you?
>
> A: Well, it was a district complaint. We discussed that it was premature to take disciplinary action against an employee without a complete investigation.
>
> Mr. Stanton: Objection, nonresponsive. (Vargas, page 120)

Let's see. The district was paying attorney's fees for the individual that Vargas claimed the district had filed a complaint against and also paying the same attorney for representing the district who claimed it filed a complaint against the teacher. Go figure! Questioning on this issue continued the following day:

> Q: Did you authorize the district legal counsel to provide a defense to (the teacher) in the SBEC matter?
>
> A: Yes, I did. I believe I did.
>
> Q: When did you do that?

A: I don't recall.

Q: Was it in the last two weeks?

A: I don't recall. I don't know—no, two weeks doesn't ring a bell. It was prior to that.

Q: It was quite a bit prior to that, wasn't it?

A: Yeah.

Q: Is that true?

A: This prior two weeks, I would have to agree. (Vargas, page 255)

This line of questioning continued on page 256:

Q: Who advises the school board on legal matters if you, as superintendent, chose to bring a disciplinary matter to the board's attention involving (the teacher)?

A: My understanding would be our legal counsel, Mr. Jones.

Q: And did you direct Mr. Jones to provide a defense to (the teacher) with the SBEC? I mean didn't that occur?

A: I wouldn't use those terms. I believe we had a discussion about the need for the district to represent (the teacher), given that up to that point, we didn't have a conclusive basis for the actions taken by the district through Dr. Durrett.

Q: Well, there is really not a conflict, then, with Mr. Jones representing (the teacher) at the SBEC and Mr. Jones advising the board on any disciplinary matter, is there?

A: Not that I am aware of.

Q: That really doesn't create a problem for you at all. Is that correct?

A: No.

Q: Well, then I'll ask it differently. Is there any conflict between having legal counsel represent or advise you and the board on disciplinary matters and represent this employee before the SBEC? Is there any conflict?

A: Not to my knowledge. I'm not aware of any.

Q: In other words, Mr. Jones' effective representation of (the teacher) would not interfere with his advice to the board on a grievance matter. Is that correct?

A: I don't believe so.

Q: You don't believe so?

A: I don't believe so. (Vargas, pages 256–257)

Q: Fine. Did you require agreement by the board for you to authorize legal counsel to represent (the teacher)?

A: I don't believe so.

Q: Would you have discussed with the board your using district resources to have a legal counsel represent (the teacher) in front of the SBEC?

A: Yes. I don't recall, though, specifically when that occurred. (Vargas, page 258)

(The teacher) confirmed this answer during his deposition in this exchange:

Q: (Teacher), have you authorized Mr. Jones to act on your behalf in connection with any of the proceedings at the State Board of Educator Certification?

A: I have... I have... Mr. Jones told me that the school district had authorized him to represent me, and I approved of that, yes. (And——, page 13)

Several board members had different ideas regarding how to characterize the (teacher) complaint origination. Was it Durrett's or the district's? Unlike Vargas, Board Member Peartree was very clear about who the complainant was regarding (the teacher). The following exchange was recorded in his deposition, on pages 9 and 10:

> Q: It was your belief that Dr. Durrett had filed a complaint against (the teacher). Is that your understanding?
>
> A: Mm-hm.
>
> Q: Is that a yes?
>
> A: Yes. That is a yes.
>
> Q: Did you think that the school district had filed a complaint against (the teacher)?
>
> A: No, I realized well, right at first I kind of thought it was. But it soon cleared up after reading it and talking to a few people that it was a complaint through a whistle-blowing agency and he had done it as an individual. (Peartree, page 10)

On March 16, 2001, almost two years after filing my complaint against Vargas, I received a phone call from a friend in El Paso (I still had a few) who told me to get a copy of the March 15, 2001, Borderland section of the *El Paso Times*. It carried the following headline: "Vargas Wins 2 Rounds, Rejoins Board." The article stated:

> The State Board of Educator Certification stopped an investigation into allegations that Vargas wrongfully fired former associate superintendent Robert Durrett.

> SBEC Spokesperson Patrick Shaughnessy said:

> This was an agreement between our legal staff and (Vargas') lawyers. It can be brought up again, but right now it is on the back burner.

In my opinion, it had never been on the front burner! Indeed, it was on the back burner. It did not seem to matter to the SBEC what their policies said or what the Administrative Code required. Their statement indicated that they were not going to take any action until my lawsuit was completed, if they acted at all. I wondered what their logic was until I read (the teacher's) deposition and learned the "why" from his answer:

> Q: Did Jones speak for you in that conversation? What did you conclude from that?
> A: The outcome was that they were going to con-template, think about what further action they would take, because they were very busy with other items as far as getting people for molesting children in the classroom and they had less time for events like mine. (Teacher, page 17)

My attorney had attended the March board meeting that evening to hear the SBEC report. After the meeting he called to fill me in on what had happened and to reassure me that my case was not over. I also received several phone calls that night from supporters who were very disturbed and wondering what I was going to do. What a blessing it was to receive encouraging words from Christian friends! The next morning, I faxed a letter to my attorney lamenting over, among other things, Shaughnessy's comment, "This was an agreement between our legal staff (SBEC) and (Vargas') lawyers."

It seemed totally immoral to me. The SBEC agreed with the perpetrator of the act (Vargas) without consulting the victim (me). *How can this be?* I thought. At the very least, I believed this action was against their standard operating procedures. It did however strengthen my belief that the district bosses were somehow connected to and applying pressure on the SBEC to reverse their decision. Once again, a decision made in Austin was not to support the whistle-blower (little old me) but to support the political power structure. Why was I not surprised?

20

A God Thing: Do You Believe in Miracles? I Do

In my past I had many occasions to deal with attorneys concerning employee issues, both as lawyers working with me and as lawyers for employees suing my employers. I came to know one local lawyer outside of district legal issues in 1993. That year I attended the Walk to Emmaus. He was the lay director for the weekend. He was also the lawyer for the parents of a student who had filed a lawsuit against the district. During the meetings and/or depositions with the board lawyers and him, I began to have great respect for the way he handled himself and the respect he showed to the individuals he deposed. He was the only lawyer I ever thought about hiring. I was blessed when he agreed that he and his partner would represent me. Now I felt confident that I was on solid ground.

So where was God during the process? Well, I believe he led me to my lawyers. Next was when the SBEC attempted to decline pursuing my (teacher) complaint. Recall that they ruled that I had filed my complaint as an *agent* of the district.

One of the consequences of this ruling was that now I could be fired for insubordination. In order to continue pursuing my complaint, my lawyers had to appeal that ruling to a three-judge review panel. It was this unbiased review panel that unanimously overturned the SBEC ruling. To me it was a miracle, *a God thing*. Finally, part of the establishment was siding with me.

Fortunately for me, Federal District Court Judge Hudspeth had also ruled on April 18, 2000, that the SBEC was wrong—another miracle, *another God thing* for me. Wow, a three-judge review panel and a federal judge were on my side!

Next, I received a second memo suspending me. You might recall that this was my formal notice of *termination for insubordination* informing me that the board would reconsider my fate at the next board meeting on November 10, 1999. Not only did they reconsider it but they voted to fire me. If the board had fired me prior to November 6, 1999, which they tried to do in September, I would have lost 30 percent of my retirement pay and be sixty years old, still bald, still have big floppy ears, and without a job. So the termination date of November 10 was a blessing, *a God thing*! My brain had been focused on the lawsuit, so I had been unaware of the good fortune of being terminated on that date.

It was a *God thing* because November 6 was the date that I completed ten years of creditable service for retirement purposes. So, if I was going to be fired, this was a date that held some great news for us. Carolyn and I had been purchasing one year of retirement credit for each completed year of service in Texas for the prior nine years. I was at home gazing at my navel and still cogitating my existence when I received the notification from the Teacher Retirement System stating that after November 6 I could purchase my twentieth year of service and my retirement would be fully vested. Needless to say, we quickly sent a check to them by return mail. *Wow!* Another *God thing*! God works in mysterious ways, his miracles to perform.

CHAPTER 21

TIME FOR MORE DEPOSITIONS: WHO'S ON FIRST?

Once I had filed my federal lawsuit, it was necessary for the discovery process to move into high gear. Of course, the school board now wanted to take my deposition. I was deposed fourteen months after my termination on January 19, 2000, from 10:03 a.m. to 5:38 p.m. Prior to my deposition, the defendants (school board's attorney, Jones) had requested that I produce many documents as a part of the discovery process.

Their defense strategy became clearer to me throughout my deposition. They questioned me on my performance prior to, during, and after Vargas's demand that I withdraw my SBEC complaint. Their questions also covered the following areas:

1. Insubordination
2. The complaint filed by the district not me
3. The district investigation being not complete

Questions by the defense's attorney did not get right to the point of my lawsuit. For example, the first questions from attorney Jones were about my age and if I had ever given a deposition before and, if I had, how many times. When I said I had given a deposition before, he wanted to know if it was because I had been sued in my official capacity or as a witness. I responded as a witness (Durrett, page 5).

Next came questions about what documents I had reviewed for my depositions. As it turned out, the following questions would figure into their defense to my lawsuit. They were:

> Q: Did you provide in this response to our request for discovery a copy of the documents that you sent to the SBEC?
>
> A: Without going through each and every one of these documents, I can't tell you. My belief is yes.
>
> Q: Your answer is yes, that the documents you provided that were attached to the complaint you filed on June 30th with the State Board of Education, that the documents that were attached to that complaint are included in either here or in the supplementation?
>
> A: I believe that is correct, but without looking at each and every one of them, I… I believe that's a correct statement.
>
> Q: Well, do you have an additional set of documents at home or anywhere else?
>
> A: No.
>
> Q: …that are…that are separate and apart from the documents that you've provided to us in our request for discovery?
>
> A: No.
>
> Q: Okay. Every document that you have that relates to the (the teacher) matter, then, you've provided us?
>
> A: That's correct, that I could find. (Durrett, pages 10–11)

And later on:

> Q: Well, Dr. Durrett, that wasn't my question.
> A: Oh, I'm sorry.
> Q: My question was did you copy those documents from the school's internal personnel file for (the teacher), the documents that you sent attached to your SBEC complaint against (the teacher)?
> A: Did I personally copy them? No.

Still later:

> Q: Okay, so was it your idea to file the complaint with the SBEC, or was it Mr. Martinez's idea?
> A: It was my idea.
> Q: Exclusively?
> A: I don't know that I discussed it with him whether or not I was going to file a complaint or not. It was my decision to file a complaint.

Following this, he asked:

> Q: Okay. What was your job title when you were working as an employee of the Ysleta Independent School District?
> A: Associate superintendent for human resources. (Durrett, pages 12–13)

From page 17 he asked:

> Q: Okay. So may I assume, then, that you're familiar with the Review Committee process?
> A: Regarding DHB?
> Q: The Review Committee process that's put in motion when there's a...an employee

> discipline matter that arises at one of the
> campuses?
>
> A: Yes.

On pages 18–19:

> Q: Okay. Did you...and you're...are you saying
> that you did not get involved in any way with
> the (teacher) Review Committee process?
>
> A: Other than accepting the information from
> Danny and him apprising me of what was
> going on. I did not meet with the committee,
> if that's what you mean, no.

Then he asked me if I had talked with any member of the committee, to which I responded "no" until he asked about speaking to Danny. I had already testified that Danny had updated me on the committee's progress (Durrett, pages 19 and 20).

The next series of questions gave me a hint about how they would try to impeach (you know, make me a liar) my testimony. Jones asked questions in which he was confusing board policy DHB and a supplemental handbook entitled *Employee Misconduct Investigation Guidelines*. I had compiled this handbook for a clinic to give administrative personnel additional ideas of how to more fully implement the regulations for board policy DHB. This guideline was not a part of the official process as described in board policy. I had never submitted it to the board for approval:

> Q: Then if you reviewed the file, then you could
> say yourself that these guidelines had been
> complied with, could you not?
>
> A: I did not say I compared the file to those
> guidelines. Those are helpful hints to—they
> are not part of policy.
>
> Q: Did you make an independent verification of
> your own that your guidelines that you wrote

in this employment handbook we're talking
about were complied with?

A: In my mind, after reviewing the documents
given to me, I believed the policy DHB had
been followed. (Durrett, pages 24–25)

Some of the questions he was asking were intended to show
that I had failed to follow policy and therefore my complaint was
flawed. He would later claim this as grounds for the superintendent
to demand that I withdraw my SBEC complaint:

Q: You said you reviewed the file. Where are the
other statements?

A: If they're not in the file, then they were not
submitted.

Q: Your rules and regulations also require that
the person taking the statements take detailed
notes to make sure important points are written down. Can you show me in this personnel
file, the (teacher) personnel file, the detailed
notes of Mr. Nava?

A: Are you reading from the guidelines in the…
in the Clinic Handbook?

Q: Yes, sir, I am.

A: Those are not policies. They're—

Q: On page four.

A: Excuse me. Those are not policies. Those are
guidelines which I issued to give principals
an idea of what to do, and supervisors, and in
doing investigations. (Durrett, page 28)

After many questions concerning whether or not I had made
sure that the clinic handbook guidelines had been followed, his questions began to focus on my knowledge of specific processes within
various board policies, apparently looking for performance issues he

could use to support my termination. In his next question he referred to me as Dr. Vargas:

> Q: Dr. Vargas (sic), are you familiar with the adage that ignorance of the law is no defense or excuse?
>
> A: I've heard the phrase, yes.
>
> Q: Well, would the same hold true of your… the district's rules and regulations and policies? The fact that you don't know them is no excuse for you violating them, would it be?
>
> A: Oh, I don't think so.
>
> Q: All right. Are you familiar with Policy—and this is a policy that directly relates to your administration of your office—DBA-R (i) (1)?
>
> A: D—, no. I'd have to review it.
>
> Q: The documents that you attached to your SBEC complaint included documents out of that personnel file, did they not?
>
> A: Out of a personnel file?
>
> Q: Out of this personnel file right here.
>
> A: I don't consider that a personnel file. It's an employee relations investigation file.
>
> Q: Well, whether you consider it one or not this is the…this is not a part of (teacher's) personnel records, what's in this file here?
>
> A: Not yet, no. May become after a decision is made. Depends on the outcome. (Durrett, pages 46–47)

He next moved to questions regarding what files I had attached to my complaint and sent to the SBEC. He appeared to be trying to establish some basis to declare that I had filed my complaint on behalf of the district:

> Q: Okay. And this is the first and only complaint you ever filed?

A: Yes, that's correct. (Durrett, page 57)

Q: You were quite anxious to have the SBEC look into the (teacher), were you not?

A: "Anxious" I'm not sure is an appropriate word.

Q: Well, Dr. (teacher) (sic), you've never filed a complaint before? You must have considered this a pretty serious matter.

A: As a matter of fact, prior to March, April of this year, I, as an individual, could not file a complaint. I was not a certified educator. I could not file a complaint. This was a whole new ball game.

Q: Right.

A: This was my first opportunity to file a complaint—

Q: Right and you—

A: ...had I wanted to. (Durrett, page 58)

His questions then moved to why I had filed this complaint but had not filed a complaint against the prior superintendent Anthony Trujillo. These questions seemed to be asked because I had previously testified in the board's termination hearing against Mr. Trujillo:

Q: Well, I'm going to assume, then, that you would consider misappropriation of public funds to be a serious matter, would you not?

A: Sure do.

Q: Did you file a complaint against Anthony Trujillo with the State Board of Educator Certification?

A: I have—a complaint was never made to me that he did that.

Q: My question was did you file a complaint?

A: No, I did not.

Q: And you know, do you not, that he was found guilty by a hearing officer in the State of Texas of misappropriating public funds?

A: I do not know that. I was not a party to that lawsuit. I was not involved in it other than as a witness. (Durrett, page 59)

Next, his questions seemed to be trying to put some evil intent behind my motive for filing the complaint:

Q: Well, in fact, you were…you were actually wanting the state agency to take action in the (teacher) matter even before you composed your draft letter to Cary Decuir on June the 14th, weren't you?

A: Wanting them to take action?

Q: Yes, sir.

A: I don't recall having that thought.

Q: You were communicating with employees at the Texas Education Agency, weren't you?

A: Asking for information.

Q: But it went deeper than that, didn't it? You were communicating with other employees at the agency about the (teacher) matter, were you not?

A: Not that I recall, no. (Durrett, pages 59–60)

Q: I asked you if you had communicated with other employees at the agency; you said you couldn't remember. Here's your letter right here. It's dated April 30th.

A: Well, forgive me for not being able to separate TEA from SBEC, but that letter was to TEA, to Mr. Moses asking a very specific question for information.

Q: Does that refresh your memory?

A: Yeah.

Q: You were trying to get the agency interested in this case before you sent the complaint to the SBEC, were you not?

A: I asked for clarification from TEA. (Durrett, page 62)

Q: The statement here that the teacher was an officer of the local teacher's organization which had endorsed Mrs. Scrivner, that's a false statement as well, is it not?

A: I believe the sentence reads "It is also reported that the teacher is an officer." I didn't know that. That's what had been reported. Mr. Crowder is the one that made the phone call and gave me the information.

Q: What do you mean "These are issues for Solomon, not me"? "I thought that Moses could at least give me advice on whether or not either issue should be pursued." Is this a religious reference?

A: It's merely trying to be lighthearted. I was just trying to say that I—whether that was on duty or not was an important issue on whether or not...what to do, and I asked for guidance.

Q: Did he answer this letter?

A: No, he did not. (Durrett, page 63)

His next few questions were very interesting because he must have believed that I had been in constant contact with someone at the SBEC in some unseemly desire to find a way to "get" the teacher:

Q: You were talking to employees at the SBEC well before you filed the complaint, were you not?

A: I don't recall personally making any phone calls to them early on, no.

Q: Dr. Durrett, in your own discovery responses, you name three people that you talked to.

A: Okay.

Q: Does that refresh your memory?

A: Early in June? No. That I talked to some of them? Yes.

Q: Cary Decuir. You talked to her. You talked to Jackie Strashun, who's the attorney at the SBEC, and you talked to Pamela Tackett. Now, does that refresh your memory?

A: Early in June? I don't believe that's when those contacts were made.

Q: Well, your phone records from your office indicate a large number of phone calls to the SBEC. I'm going to assume you were making those calls, Dr. Durrett, unless you tell me some other employee, then I would like to know that person's name.

Mr. Antcliff: I'd like to see the records—

The witness: Me too.

Mr. Antcliff: ...if I could have those.

Mr. Jones: I don't have the records with me— (By Mr. Jones) Are you I'm asking you did you make a number of calls, and when I say "a number," I'm not talking about two or three. I'm talking about dozens—

A: Oh, no.

Q: ...of phone calls?

A: No.

Q: So if your phone records indicate that there were dozens of calls made to the SBEC, are you testifying you did not make those calls?

A: Were they made from my extension?

Q: I believe they were.

> A: I... I don't believe that's an accurate descrip-
> tion, because I don't believe I made that many
> calls. (Durrett, pages 65–66)

As it turned out the calls he was trying to attribute to me were actually made by the certification clerk in my office to the certification division of the SBEC.

His next line of questions seemed to be attempting to prove that I knew I was insubordinate by not requesting permission to file a complaint with the SBEC:

> Q: Why...why—during this period of time that
> you were going through all this thought pro-
> cess—why didn't you... I'll be more specific.
> Why didn't you talk to Dr. Vargas and tell
> him that you were contemplating filing a
> complaint with the State Board of Educator
> Certification and that you were talking to
> employees at the SBEC and that you had
> written a letter to the Commissioner of
> Education? Did you tell him that you wrote
> a letter to Commissioner Moses?
> A: I don't know whether I mentioned it or not.
> Didn't copy him on that one.
> Q: No, you didn't. Why didn't you—
> A: Well, he wasn't even here then. (Durrett, pages
> 65–66)

Similar questioning continued:

> Q: You didn't feel any obligation to talk to your
> immediate superior, the superintendent,
> about your planned action?
> A: Obligation?
> Q: Yes, sir.
> A: No. Not at that point, no.

> Q: Or the fact that you were going to file a com-
> plaint against an employee before an inves-
> tigation was even completed by the District
> Review Committee?
> A: I believe at that point there was an admission
> by (the teacher) that that had occurred.
> Q: And at no time did you ever consider talking
> to your immediate supervisor about…your
> plans to file a complaint with SBEC?
> A: Sent him a copy of it. (Durrett, pages 67–68)

At this point the questions by Mr. Jones seemed to move toward proving that I had failed to follow SBEC regulations requiring the complaint be sent to the superintendent by certified mail:

> Q: You sent your letter by certified mail, correct?
> You sent it on June the 30th?
> A: I believe that's correct.
> Q: You continued to work here until August
> the 10th, correct? That is the date of your
> suspension?
> A: I believe that's correct.
> Q: And since you sent the letter, okay, the green
> card would be expected to come back to the
> sender, correct?
> A: Normally, yes.
> Q: So where is the green card?
> A: Well, I believe they were sent by Danny
> Martinez, if you look at the receipt, so… I
> believe they're initialed DM, so they may be
> in employee relations. (Durrett, page 69)
> Q: Yeah, but did the envelope did the return
> receipt have return to Bob Durrett?
> A: I don't know how he filled them out. (Durrett,
> page 69)
> Q: Well, who sent the letter?

A: I typed, signed the letter. It was mailed by Mr.
Martinez. (Durrett, page 70)

Questions became more specific. He now moved toward trying
to show that I could not have filed the complaint with the SBEC as
an individual because of the time, place, and letterhead paper which
I used to prepare the complaint:

Q: And this letter was prepared while you were
in the course and scope of your employment
with the Ysleta Independent School District,
correct?

A: Correct.

Q: And using district resources and staff?

A: Correct.

Q: Both to prepare the correspondence and to
mail it?

A: Correct. (Durrett, page 71)

Questions then moved toward what Administrative Code or
Penal Code which I thought might have been violated by the teacher.

Q: In many of the (teacher) documents, reports
and memorandums and so forth, there are
references to the possibility that (the teacher)
had engaged in some kind of conduct that
was a violation of the Texas Penal Code, right?

A: I believe that's correct.

Q: Well, go ahead and just tell me the general
provisions of the...of that part of the penal
code that you believe was violated by (the
teacher)?

A: I didn't say I believe they were violated. I
believe the allegations were there that it had
occurred, and they included bribing his students to participate in an election for a sitting

board member and a candidate. And I have
no idea what he was to get in return. That
was never ever determined.

Q: You don't...you don't really believe that he
engaged in any kind of bribery yourself, do
you?

A: I don't know what the agreement was. I do not
know what went on. (Durrett, pages 71–72)

Later on he moved to specific questions regarding my lawsuit
against the district and Vargas:

Q: Dr. Durrett, this is a copy of your original
complaint that was filed in your lawsuit that
commenced these legal proceedings. Did you
have a chance to review it with you attorney
before it was filed?

A: I'm sure I did.

Q: Can you tell me whether or not you are alleging in your lawsuit that your rights to free
speech were violated?

A: Yes, I believe that's correct.

Q: Okay. Tell me how Dr. Vargas violated your
right to free speech.

A: He instructed me to withdraw my complaint
to the State Board for Educator Certification.
(Durrett, pages 86–87)

Q: Yes. Okay. The school district has never told
you, instructed you, given you any written
communication, verbal communication, or
any type of communication telling you that
you could not exercise your rights to free
speech in any context, other than one you
just mentioned, has it?

A: No. They just fired me for it. (Durrett, page
90)

Another defense centered on their assertion that, by my filing a complaint, I had created a hostile work environment in the district or that I had undermined the authority of the superintendent by telling some folks or a lot of folks I had filed a complaint:

> Q: Since you filed the complaint with the SBEC, have you ever attempted to talk about the subject matter of the (teacher) complaint or anything implicated in the (teacher) complaint with any person or group of persons, other than your legal counsel?
>
> A: That I have reached out to, no. (Durrett, page 92)

This line of questioning continued in the assumption that, if I considered my constitutional rights violated, it would be of such an affront that I would be telling every person I knew:

> Q: Okay. So we agree, then, that a violation of your constitutional right is something that rises to a high level of importance?
>
> A: Yes.
>
> Q: Substantial dimensions?
>
> A: Yes.
>
> Q: And would you agree with me that any person such as yourself, similarly situated, who suffered such a violation would be quick to inform those who are close to him about the nature of the violation?
>
> A: I'm sorry. One more time. You lost me.
>
> Q: Dr. Durrett, let me put it to you this way: If you got robbed today at gunpoint, you'd probably tell somebody about it, wouldn't you?
>
> A: Most likely.
>
> Q: Right.

A: I'd report it.

Q: And we've already agreed that a violation of your constitutional right is a matter of...of extreme importance to you, okay? Have we agreed on that?

A: That a violation of constitutional rights is extremely important to me?

Q: Yes, sir.

A: Yes.

Q: And probably if someone assaulted you, you would tell somebody about it.

A: Would depend on the assault.

Q: Uh-huh. Can you give me the names of every person with whom you have discussed in detail the violation of your constitutional rights that you allege in your lawsuit?

A: My wife in a very limited way. My lawyer, Mr. Stanton.

Q: Okay.

A: I might have my brother. Might have with another brother, but I don't... I don't recall going out and making an issue of this to anybody except people I thought was the appropriate people. (Durrett, pages 97–98)

The following questions seemed to stem from the Trujillo termination hearing. The questions generally centered on whether or not I applied district policy consistently or turned a blind eye to some other wrongdoings. His questions referenced notes which I had made in my time management calendar:

Q: I would like to—do you think that this was just copied poorly, that if we got the original again, that we...we could get a better copy of it?

A: It could be easier to read. I can probably make out most of it, but—

Q: Yes.

A: The second one also was it says, "TEA, so you're not withdrawing your complaint? No." And oh, this was a conversation that I had with Dr. Vargas. He said, "So you are not withdrawing your complaint?" And I told him no. And because he had directed me, I have filed a complaint against him also.

Q: Because you direct me I have filed a complaint against you?

A: "Well, it looks like we have a problem then" was his response. (Durrett, page 122)

Q: Can you read the next sentence?

A: "Asked" if something…"asked if I'd do same for buses being used to campaign," and I said, "same."

Q: Yeah, but you never…you never filed an SBEC complaint against anybody, so obviously you never filed a complaint against any district employee for using buses for campaign purposes?

A: Did not have the authority until just recently, that's correct. Didn't have the right.

Q: But you…you never made a report of that conduct to any person, did you?

A: Whose conduct? This was a question to me. I don't know whose conduct he was talking about.

Q: Using buses for campaign purposes?

A: Who used the buses for campaign purposes? I—he didn't say someone had done that. It could have been a hypothetical.

> Q: And you don't have any information or knowl-
> edge of any district employee ever using a bus
> for campaign purposes?
> A: An allegation of that nature has never been
> brought to my attention.
> Q: No one's ever discussed that with you?
> A: An allegation has never been brought to my
> attention. (Durrett, page 123)

Questions regarding whether or not I had discussed my lawsuit with other individuals continued. Apparently, he was still searching for information to buttress their defense that I had disrupted the management operations of the district:

> Q: Who are the people, sir, that you talked to?
> A: Oh, mercy. I didn't keep a list, but other than
> Jan, I believe Vern Butler called. Lilly Limon
> called. Tony Trujillo called. I know there was
> a couple others, but I just don't recall who
> they were.
> Q: Tony Trujillo's a friend of yours, isn't he?
> A: No.
> Q: Okay. He's an acquaintance?
> A: Yes.
> Q: You told me one time, Dr. Durrett, that you
> don't socialize with the people that work for
> the school district. Do you remember telling
> me that?
> A: As a matter of fact, that's a true statement.
> (Durrett, page 146)

From there he began questioning me about my allegations of improper harassment of me by Vargas. He was continuing to ask questions related to entries I had made in my time management calendar:

Q: You charge that Superintendent Vargas engaged in a campaign of harassment by setting unreasonable time deadlines on work tasks. And you've made one reference here just a minute ago to the Diederich matter. That he made critical, demeaning statements to you and...about your performance, okay? And that failing to follow school policies related to employment matters and that he intentionally overtaxed the resources of the human resources department. So I want to ask you about references to all those. Do you understand?

A: I'll do my best.

Q: Okay.

A: I'm at 264 now, if that's helpful.

Q: Okay.

A: He's telling me that he wants to bring in people without advertising. He wants the level to the job to jump to the executive level on Bolanos. He wanted to make sure human resources should not have—he says we should not have allowed a press conference. Told him it had nothing to do with employee relations or HR. In one breath, he says central office is top-heavy. In the next breath, he says create two more senior positions.

Q: Now, what is that a reference to? Is that, you know, I'd asked you about things that relate to...

A: Kind of unreasonable, I think, to ask me not to follow policy.

Q: I had asked you about unreasonable time deadlines, making critical, demeaning statements, failing to follow school polices related

to employment matters, and intentionally
overtaxing the resources.

A: Telling me I should not have allowed a press
conference. Had nothing to do with the press
conference.

Q: Is this the press conference where Lucy Araujo
revealed confidential personnel matters to
the public?

A: I don't know whether she revealed confidential
matters or not. That's the press conference he
is referring to. (Durrett, page 149)

During this same time frame, it seemed to me that the board
must have started doubting the legal advice they were receiving
from Mr. Jones. Even though the board had fired my old boss, Tony
Trujillo, in December of 1998, he must have still been on the minds
of some board members because on the October 23, 2000, board
agenda, item no. 6 was to:

Review and take appropriate action with
respect to formal arbitration proposal re: Trujillo
vs. YISD.

I was not privy to the reasons that they would be going into
arbitration with him, but apparently something had been "amiss"
with the legal issues in his 1998 termination hearing which had been
handled by Mr. Jones.

Also, at this meeting item no. 18 on the consent agenda was to:

Approve an engagement letter effective
February 1, 2000, with Mounce, Green, Myers,
Safi & Galatzan for work referred by Luther
Jones and/or Dr. Edward Lee Vargas. (Page 27)

Apparently, this item created someone some consternation because a board member pulled it from the October 23, 2000, consent agenda. Someone did not want to continue their services.

Later, in reviewing board minutes, I learned of their "retroactive" hiring and termination. The November 8, 2000 minutes contained a motion on page 2:

> Item No. 4: Approve an engagement letter effective February 1, 2000, with Mounce, Green, Myers, Safi & Galatzan for work referred by Luther Jones and/or Dr. Edward Lee Vargas. Trustee Sanchez made a motion to pay this firm up to whatever the District owes them and terminate the contract... Item was approved.

Approving a contract after the work was completed seemed to be a little out of the ordinary. Oh, well, it was not the only thing that seemed weird in my case.

Interesting! One could speculate that Jones had been hiring additional legal help without board authority but with at least some belief that the board would eventually approve his actions.

But what the heck? They were elected officials, and I guess they could do whatever they wanted until someone had the courage to take them to task.

I wondered if the board realized that they were now going into arbitration with Trujillo on the probability that legal advice they received from Jones was not accurate.

At their December 13, 2000, meeting, the district accepted the arbitrator's recommended settlement agreement with Mr. Trujillo two years after the board fired him. I was not privy to the terms of his settlement. But, of course, he was fired before I was; so it appeared that they were getting rid of old legal matters first.

My, my, the board was moving much faster on settling their arbitration negotiations with my old boss than they were in getting my case to trial. Oh, well, I had to keep moving.

My attorneys had taken the deposition of Dr. Vargas on portions of January 18 and 19 and February 10 of 2000. So I was now aware of his *positions on why he wanted me fired.*

One defense raised by Dr. Vargas was that my failure to withdraw the complaint was causing him difficulty in managing the district. Here are his responses to a couple of questions:

> Q: I want to take you now to your affidavit, Exhibit 22. You've indicated at paragraph 19 that Robert Durrett's refusal to withdraw the complaint with the SBEC was made known to other senior management employees. Do you see that? Paragraph 19, the bottom of page 4 and top of page 5.
>
> A: Say that again?
>
> Q: Do you see that?
>
> A: Yes.
>
> Q: Can you tell me the name of any senior management employees who knew of Dr. Durrett's refusal to withdraw the SBEC complaint?
>
> A: I'd have to go back to my notes and see who may have been involved in any of these related discussions. I know, for example, my administrative assistant, Lupe McVay. I know that people talk around here and everybody... I'm assuming whoever handled the documents on Dr. Durrett's end as far as his staff. (Vargas, pages 201–202)

He had made several assumptions regarding how I had processed the complaint and was not aware that I had not discussed it with any employee of the district and, therefore, it could not have had any impact on the operations of the district. It later became apparent when he responded with several answers. I have quoted only two of his answers:

Q: Dr. Vargas, is it your testimony that you don't know the name of any management employee who knew in July and August 1999 that Dr. Durrett was refusing to withdraw his complaint?

A: I'd have to go back to look at my notes.

Q: And from your recollection today, you don't know of any person, do you?

A: Well, I'm trying to recall back—this is quite a while back—who all was involved in the discussions. Danny Martinez and others who were involved were aware. I know that board members were aware and there was a lot of discussion around the district about it, rumors, that type of thing. (Vargas, pages 202–203)

Further questions regarding who told whom went like this:

Q: Who told board members that Dr. Durrett had failed to withdraw the complaint to the SBEC? Was that (the teacher)? Was that Edward Vargas?

A: I had told the board that I had asked him to withdraw the complaint.

Q: When did you tell the board that? Did you tell them in open session or executive session, or did you tell them in a written memorandum?

A: I believe I told them through a written memorandum or week-in review. I'd have to go back and check. (Vargas, page 203)

Q: When did you inform them and in what forum?

A: I don't recall, but I do know that when I made a recommendation to the board for termination, I did inform them the reasons why. (Vargas, pages 203–204)

Discovering his assertion as to what disruption I had caused in his ability to manage the district and when it occurred was elusive as evidenced by the following question:

> Q: I take it from the executive session tapes that have been provided to me and we've listened to, it is prior to September 10 you did not have an executive session meeting pardon me, prior to August 10, you did not inform the board in executive session that an employee was being insubordinate, did you?
>
> A: I don't recall. I know that the first time we discussed it as a board was during the executive session.
>
> Q: Right. And the executive session had to do with after you suspended Dr. Durrett?
>
> A: Yes.
>
> Q: So look again at Exhibit 22, paragraph 19, at the top of page 5 for me, would you? Can you tell me how any board member or any senior staff member knew that Dr. Durrett had been insubordinate prior to your decision to suspend Dr. Durrett?
>
> A: Well, there were a lot of—as I stated earlier—a lot of talk going around and rumors and such. And I could not have a senior employee, my associate superintendent, failing to comply with a directive and repeatedly, after asking him to reconsider, denying that request. I would lose my ability to run the district if my top senior staff were insubordinate and not complying with directives. (pages 205–206)

So the question was still lingering as to who was causing the disruption among the staff, me or someone else. So the questions continued:

Q: Is it possible that you were the one that was telling board members and staff members that Dr. Durrett had failed to follow your direction to withdraw the complaint?

A: It's possible.

Q: So in that regard, is it fair to say that Dr. Durrett didn't directly undermine your authority by reporting to other people his insubordination?

A: He undermined my authority by refusing a directive.

Q: But you're not here to say under oath that Dr. Durrett caused any of that information to get out beyond your memos to him and his responses to you?

A: I don't know. I don't know if he did or not.

Q: And you didn't know when you terminated him whether or not he had caused any of that information to get out?

A: No. (Vargas, page 208)

So he could not recall any instance in which I had discussed my complaint with any person who had directly affected his management of the district employees.

Next, my wonderful lawyers moved on to another of his stated reasons for my dismissal:

Q: And that wasn't the reason you terminated him. You terminated him for refusal to follow your direction. Is that correct?

A: Exactly, by that refusal undermining my ability to manage this district when a top associate superintendent is not willing to comply with a directive. (Page 208)

CHAPTER 22

WHAT DID HE KNOW AND WHEN DID HE KNOW IT?

My lawyers then moved to questions regarding whether or not Vargas was aware that I had the right to file a complaint with a state agency. Questions concerning his "awareness" brought about some interesting responses. This series of questions went like this:

> Q: Now, you have, in connection with your work here at the school district, been involved in assisting to give notice to employees that retaliation is prohibited by state law?
>
> A: Yes.
>
> Q: I show you Exhibit 39, a copy of the notice to employees that's posted prominently around this building, isn't it?
>
> A: Yes, it is.
>
> Q: And is it your view that you would condone or not condone the conduct of any supervisor of employees retaliating against them?
>
> A: Not condone.
>
> Q: You would not condone it?

A: Not condone retaliation.

Q: That's very serious, isn't it?

A: Absolutely.

Q: How serious is it to retaliate against an employee for reporting in good faith an allegation of violation of state law?

A: Can you restate that?

Q: Are there some kinds of violations of state law that are so serious that we should not discourage the reporting of those violations?

A: We should not discourage the reporting of the violations. (Vargas, pages 209–210)

Q: Were you familiar, in general, with the requirements to not retaliate against employees for making a report to law enforcement? Were you familiar with that in August 1999?

A: Yes.

Q: You were aware prior to recommending to the board termination of Dr. Durrett that it was Dr. Durrett's contention that the suspension by you was in retaliation for his making a complaint to the SBEC and refusing to withdraw it?

A: I was aware that... I became aware of his complaint after the decision to suspend and recommend termination, and...

Q: Because that decision was on August 10, 1999?

A: I have to go back and look at the exact date. (Vargas, pages 211–212)

Fortunately for me, the dates in the documents spoke for themselves; and he had now admitted retaliation was inappropriate. So my lawyers moved on.

Because he had alleged that I had failed to notify him and purposely concealed from him that I had filed the complaint, my lawyers followed up with these questions:

> Q: You stated in your affidavit and in the answer filed in this case that Dr. Durrett did not give you notice of the filing of his complaint against (the teacher) at the SBEC. Do you recall that?
>
> A: Yes.
>
> Q: Is it your testimony here today, that based on what you know here today, that Dr. Durrett did not give you notice after he filed the complaint of what he had done?
>
> A: My recollection of the matter is he did not give me notice prior to him filing the complaint, but he did acknowledge, when we talked about it after the fact.
>
> Q: And he gave you a copy then?
>
> A: At some point I received a copy. I don't recall exactly when. (Vargas, page 225)

Once again I was blessed by the dates on the documents and did not need to rely on his memory or mine to prove that I complied with the SBEC rules for filing a complaint. The postal number of the receipt for certified mail which was mailed to Dr. Vargas was #Z1 447 223 288 dated June 30, 1999. The initials DM on the receipt signified that Danny Martinez had mailed the forms to him.

CHAPTER 23

ALMOST THROUGH ASKING QUESTIONS AND I THOUGHT THE END WAS IN SIGHT!

The year 2001 proved to be a good year for me compared to the past two. From the time I filed my complaint, legal motions and counter-motions and delay after delay were the order of the day.

In their appeal documents, the defendants listed sixty-nine separate legal documents as having been previously processed from the time I had filed the lawsuit and their appeal. *And* we were not through. As I revisited what had happened, I was convinced that some of the board members were using every legal avenue available to push me to my limits, financially and emotionally. I was very fortunate because I had a wonderful wife, an uplifting pastor, and a faith community supporting me every day.

I was totally confused and amazed at the number of motions and at the reams of paper that were being consumed in this process. It made me wish I had bought stock in a paper mill!

In the January 30, 2001, issue of the *Times*, I finally found out why my old boss Tony Trujillo was mentioned in the December 13, 2000, board agenda. The *Times* story began:

> Trustee Charles Peartree said he doesn't want to involve the Ysleta Independent School District in the defamation lawsuit that former Superintendent Anthony Trujillo filed against him earlier this month.

In another paragraph the article stated:

> Trujillo, who also doesn't want district resources used in the suit, filed a similar lawsuit against Trustee Ronda Scrivner, who could not be reached for comment.

As you can see from this one report, the board was fractured; but I was still in their sights. I was now living in New Mexico, and my lawyers were aware that my patience and funds were dwindling. So, when they asked me about seeking a settlement with the district, I agreed. After receiving Judge Hudspeth's order on February 27, 2001, they sent a request to the board and their attorneys. The letter was addressed to the president of the board and the law firm which had been handling my case. The letter was for the purpose of engaging in settlement discussions.

Now that the board had seen the offer of judgment form and the trial date was not far away, I was hopeful that the pressure of a trial date would help bring things to a close.

My guys made the following two points regarding the status of my case to open the negotiations:

> 1. As you are aware, the U.S. District Court in El Paso, in passing on the issues relating to Dr. Vargas' qualified immunity, made specific findings which seals the fate of YISD

and Dr. Vargas on the liability issues relative to Dr. Durrett's termination. Whereas previous counsel Luther Jones argued that Dr. Durrett's speech was not public speech, *the Federal Judge here in El Paso and the U.S. Court of Appeals for the Fifth Circuit have now ruled that Dr. Durrett's speech was public speech as a matter of law.* Whereas previous counsel argued that Dr. Durrett was acting on behalf of the District when he filed his complaint against (the teacher) with the SBEC, *the Federal Judge here in El Paso and the Fifth Circuit have now ruled, as a matter of law, that Dr. Durrett's speech was both public and private, and that he was entitled to individual protection regardless of his public employment status.* Whereas previous counsel argued that Durrett's speech was disruptive of the efficient operations of the District and therefore was underserving of constitutional protection, *the Federal Judge in El Paso and the Fifth Circuit have now overruled this position by finding that there was no such disruption.* Not one of these issues will be heard by the jury in this case because they have each been decided as a matter of law against the District. As a result, the sole remaining issue is whether the cause of Dr. Durrett's termination was his refusal to withdraw the complaint.

2. Board Members Charles Peartree and Ronda Scrivner have both testified that insubordination was the reason provided to them and the reason that they voted to terminate Dr. Durrett. Dr. Durrett has every expectation that each of the other board members will

testify to the same. Superintendent Vargas
testified that the main reason for the termination was Dr. Durrett's "insubordination"
when Dr. Durrett refused Dr. Vargas's directive to withdraw the complaint. *The Fifth
Circuit found that Dr. Vargas had absolutely
no authority to direct Dr. Durrett to withdraw the complaint, and further Dr. Vargas
was charged with knowing the law surround-
ing his conduct in this area.*

The response to my offer to enter into negotiations with the
board was responded to by Vargas's personal lawyer on March 1,
2001. The first paragraph stated:

I am in receipt of your correspondence
dated February 27 addressed to Jerry Wallace and
Ismael Legarreta. As you may know, my Firm is
now only representing Dr. Vargas in this suit.
The Board of Trustees for the Ysleta Independent
School District is represented by Jerry Wallace.

In the body of the letter, it, of course, attempted to refute the
points laid out by my lawyer. Consequently, my lawyer responded to
his rebuttal; and the paperwork kept on flowing.

As the delays continued, I was thankful that I had joined a wonderful church in New Mexico and still had my supporters in El Paso
urging me on with their prayers and phone calls.

Thankfully, the *El Paso Times* continued to cover my lawsuit. I
did not attend the March 2, 2001, board meeting; so I depended on
their reports to stay informed. They reported:

Members of the board minority faction
claim that Trustee Roberto Lerma was wrong
in distributing a settlement letter from Stanton
and Antcliff, the law firm representing former

Associate Superintendent Robert Durrett in a multimillion-dollar lawsuit against suspended Superintendent Edward Lee Vargas and the district.

Actually the "settlement letter" they were referring to was my offer to enter negotiations.

During this time frame, the school board was in such disarray that the Department of Education had appointed a master to oversee their actions. At this board meeting, they were considering the reinstatement of Vargas as superintendent. The *Times* quoted the master:

I didn't want to talk about the specifics of the settlement, just acknowledge that the settlement offer had been received... I thought it would impact the decision that they would make on his employment.

I understood this quote to mean that the board did not want to discuss my settlement involving Vargas because it might prejudice their vote regarding his reinstatement.

CHAPTER 24

"THEN YOU WILL KNOW THE TRUTH AND THE TRUTH WILL SET YOU FREE" (JOHN 8:32)

March 30, 2001, was a good day for me because I learned that Judge Hudspeth had finally set my case for trial on June 4, 2001. Once again, the end appeared to be at hand.

In his letter giving me this good news, my lawyer also informed me that the attorney for Vargas was considering raising a new defense called "reliance on counsel" because of the advice Vargas had received from Luther Jones. My thoughts harkened back to my original recommendation to Vargas to remove Jones and hire another attorney for the district.

In preparation for submitting a settlement offer to the board on May 9, the attorneys for the board had apparently submitted the offer to the board for information, because on March 31, 2001, the *Times* used the phrase "settlement offer" in reporting on the happenings at the board meeting. The article stated:

> Tuesday's settlement offer came after the U.S. 5th Circuit Court of Appeals upheld a U.S. district court's decision not to grant Vargas immunity from being sued in this case and strengthened Durrett's case.

On the April 11, 2001, board agenda, under *items added after agenda was printed*, item 35 was listed as:

> Consider and act on settlement proposal in
> Durrett v. YISD & Vargas. (Sanchez)

As a result of this discussion, the board's attorney contacted my guys to talk about the settlement. My hopes continued to fluctuate from being optimistic to "my goodness what's next" after my lawyers contacted me to tell me that the board had considered a settlement offer. Was it now over? Nope! But now negotiations were beginning in earnest because the June 4 trial date was looming closer every day.

On April 17, 2001, my lawyers informed me we had finalized the wording of a settlement agreement, *but* (seems there was always one more thing) the district's lawyer wanted to wait until the impending board election was over to submit it for approval.

My case seemed to be moving along, but my original complaints to the SBEC were still languishing somewhere in the bowels of that agency.

On April 23, 2001, Vargas's law firm, Mounce, Green, and Myers, was still working away trying to find something to buttress their client's case. They wanted to retake my deposition. My response was:

> Plaintiff will not willingly do anything to
> reopen discovery or waive the opportunity to
> object to untimely discovery.

Consequently, I was not deposed a second time.

On May 9, 2001, a couple of the board's attorneys called my guys to see if I would be willing to enter into mediation. This appeared to be a final attempt to move forward based upon the settlement offer. I said yes to this inquiry.

Now it would be up to the board if they wanted to avoid going to trial. That evening's board agenda item no. 14 was:

> Consider and act on settlement and/or take
> action to limit potential damages in Durrett v.

YISD in the U.S. District Court, as discussed in
closed session.

The vote of approval was unanimous which meant that board
member Scrivner also voted in favor of not going to trial. I wondered
why the "spark plug" (as Mr. Peartree called her in his deposition)
behind terminating my contract was now willing to mediate.

The YISD board had voted to mediate! For me it was *another
God thing.* In my opinion the new lawyers finally convinced the
board that they were on the losing side if they went to trial.

The next day, May 10, the board's attorneys sent me "an offer
of settlement." The first paragraph contained the following language:

> We make this offer without any admis-
> sion of wrongdoing on behalf of any of the
> Defendants and would offer to make these pay-
> ments in exchange for a full and final release of all
> Defendants for all damages, litigation expenses
> and attorney's fees arising out of the termination
> of Dr. Durrett as Associate Superintendent of the
> Ysleta Independent School District to be included
> in a comprehensive settlement agreement.

In addition, the letter contained their first financial offer.
The first paragraph of my lawyer's response was:

> In the course of earlier negotiations on behalf
> of our respective clients, the District obtained a
> significant discount from what Plaintiff considered
> the damages obtainable at trial to be in this case.
> The District's offer of settlement is so far lower
> than our earlier discussions that it seems to invite
> a retreat by Dr. Durrett in his bargaining position.

And they concluded by saying that our original settlement offer
would remain open until Tuesday, May 15.

Much more important to me than this "lowball" offer was the second paragraph of my response:

> Dr. Durrett does not agree to release Dr. Vargas from liability without an admission from Dr. Vargas or a declaration of his culpability in directly violating Dr. Durrett's constitutional rights. Dr. Durrett's position is rock solid. If Dr. Vargas feels confident about his position on the facts and law, and if he believes that the Fifth Circuit was in error in its preliminary rulings, Dr. Vargas can litigate that issue at trial—separate from the District.

Now that the mediation process had begun, I was once again hopeful that my lawsuit would soon be over and my bank account would not continue to dwindle. At this point, we had already expended over 125,000 dollars on legal fees. So the pressure was on to make a deal that did not compromise my position regarding Vargas's violation of my rights.

I believe my faith had been preparing me for this event during the past forty-five years. After I had returned to the church, we decided to begin tithing 10 percent of our income monthly and regularly investing in our future. That was the only reason we had the financial resources to pursue my lawsuit. In retrospect, I believe there are not many folks who could have afforded to take a chance on winning a whistle-blower case, so they don't.

Good news kinda arrived on May 11 when the district sent me a counteroffer in the form of an "offer of judgment" to consider.

The phrase "offer of judgment" put a new twist on my thinking regarding the mediation process. During the mediation process, the board wanted to omit any admission of wrongdoing on the part of Vargas or the board. When this second offer was first presented to me, it contained a new dollar amount which was satisfactory to me.

However, I rejected it because it still contained language regarding the release of liability which I had already rejected. One major reason for my filing this complaint on behalf of the parents was to highlight a code of ethics violation. What benefit was it to the parents, to me, or to other employees to say that Vargas and the board had done nothing wrong? I might be stubborn, but I believed it would send a wrong signal to anyone else who might be considering filing a whistle-blower complaint. So I rejected this offer even though it contained a satisfactory dollar amount. We continued to negotiate.

Next, the district filed the *offer of judgment* form with the court on May 17, 2001, with their final offer. Now the settlement process was in my lap. The good news was that they were offering an amount acceptable to me. The not-so-good news was that the offer included the following:

> In the event of your failure to accept this offer, please be aware that should the Plaintiff recover a judgment, which is less favorable than this offer, Plaintiff shall not be entitled to any attorney's fees or costs from the date of this offer, and Defendants shall be entitled to recover as part of its cost, its attorney's fees, cost and expert witness fees from and after the date of this offer.

As a practical matter I now had to decide if I would accept their offer or go to trial. This meant that if I declined the offer and went to trial and the jury awarded me less than their last offer, I would be out even more attorneys' fees (mine and theirs) and any additional court costs.

My original intent was to expose the unethical conduct, recover what I would have earned if I had continued to work until I was sixty-five, retire, and begin drawing my Social Security and retirement. Their offer would pay me for my attorney's fees and what I would have earned if I had continued to work until I was sixty-five. The important part was that it did not contain language releasing the board or Vargas of liability. As I have heard many times, "A bird in the hand is worth two in the bush"; so I accepted their *offer of judgment.*

Now the ball was back in the hands of the board for final approval. The board approved the document on May 18, 2001. The judgment was signed by the judge on May 21 and was filed with the court on May 22, 2001. My battle with the board was over. "Is anyone happy? Let them sing songs of praise" (James 5:13).

The meaning of the phrase "offer of judgment" became an issue during the May 18, 2001, board meeting. The *Times* reported Vargas's attorney, Neal Adams, as saying the following:

> This matter is settled and it's now behind us.
> There is no admission of any liability on behalf of
> the district or Vargas.

Later in the article the *Times* reported:

> Instead of a settlement, the district and
> Vargas signed off on an Offer of Judgment, which
> held them liable for Durrett's claims that his con-
> stitutional rights were violated when he was fired.

But the board just would not give up trying to avoid publicly admitting what had happened. The *Times* reported their attempt this way:

> The board voted 4-3 on a proclamation stat-
> ing that neither the board nor Vargas intended to
> claim any liability in the case.

It did not matter what the board's intent was. Consequently, the *Times* article reported the following:

> Chris Antcliff, one of Durrett's attorneys,
> said that the proclamation has no legal meaning
> and that the Offer of Judgment still stands as the
> official closure of litigation.

The entire wording (with the exception of the dollar amount of my award) of the Judgment said: Before this Court is the notice of the parties that Defendants have offered judgment on the pleadings to Plaintiff pursuant to Rule 68 of the Federal Rules of Civil Procedure in the amount of (X dollars). Plaintiff has accepted the offer pursuant to Rule 68 in a timely manner. Accordingly, it is ORDERED, ADJUDGED AND DECREED that Judgment is entered for Plaintiff in the amount of (X dollars). And that this sum includes all costs, fees, expenses incurred by the Plaintiff. SIGNED AND ENTERED, This the 21st day of May 2001.

Finally, I thought, *My lawsuit has been finalized, and I could move on.* So was it really over for me? As someone once said, "It all depends." What happened to that original simple two-paragraph complaint that started this process? What had the SBEC done with their investigation?

As previously stated, the SBEC had informed me earlier that they would not proceed on either my teacher's or Vargas complaints until the US Court of Appeals for the Fifth Circuit had ruled on Dr. Vargas's appeal relative to his claim of qualified immunity.

So on June 4, 2001, my attorneys forwarded a copy of the offer of judgment to the SBEC requesting that my complaints be reinstated. The document had been signed by the judge on May 21, 2001, and filed with the US District Court clerk on May 22, 2001. Now I believed the investigation into my complaints would move on.

On June 27, 2001, an SBEC attorney requested a lot of additional information concerning the teacher's complaint. The information was supplied, and we continued to wait.

On July 20, 2001, I was notified by the SBEC staff attorney that the teacher's hearing had finally been scheduled and my presence was requested. In responding, my lawyer said that I would be available. He also supplied additional information to questions that had been raised by SBEC attorneys in a June 27 letter pertaining to my Vargas complaint. Apparently, a Vargas attorney was continuing to state that the offer of judgment was a release by me of Vargas from all liability. Our response was:

> Early in the week, there had been a settlement where Vargas and the School District offered to settle the case in return for a broad form release. That offer was rejected. If Vargas or his attorney is telling you that what occurred in El Paso was a settlement and a release without admitting liability, he is misleading you.

He also explained that, after the offer of judgment was approved by the board, they subsequently passed a resolution stating that they did not "intend to admit anything on behalf of Vargas or the board." Vargas's attorney was now using this argument before the SBEC. Once again, my lawyers pointed out that the resolution had no legal standing.

While the Vargas complaints remained stagnant, eventually a hearing was held in El Paso on February 12 and 13, 2002, regarding the teacher. The judge presiding over the hearing issued a recommendation on May 8, 2002, that all teaching certificates and all endorsements held by the teacher be inscribed with a reprimand for the actions taken. On August 2, 2002, his recommendation was accepted by the SBEC.

Now I wanted to know about the "other" complaints, *my* complaints regarding Vargas. On July 19, 2002, I filed an open records request of all correspondence between the SBEC or its agents or staff and the hearing officer, any other state agency including the Texas Education Agency (TEA), and the school district or its agents or representatives, Luther Jones, or Vargas. I also requested copies of all pleadings, motions, or filings with SBEC.

The information I received contained a letter from an attorney representing Vargas. It contained some interesting assertions, such as falsely stating that the offer of judgment I signed, once entered, would:

> ...fully and finally resolve(s) the claims and causes of action asserted by Durrett in the Federal Lawsuit.

In a separate paragraph they raised the board motion in which they stated they did not intend to admit any liability. They went on to raise the allegation that Vargas had received and relied on advice from Luther Jones and, therefore, had no personal responsibility.

In a separate letter dated that same day, my attorneys requested a written reply explaining the basis the SBEC utilized in terminating, resolving, or dismissing my complaint regarding Vargas. The final paragraph stated:

> Dr. Durrett to this day stands ready, willing and able to proceed as a witness and as a complaining party. He protests any action to terminate the complaint against Mr. Vargas for any reason other than consideration of the merits of the complaint.

These attempts to restart my complaints against Vargas were to no avail as no action was ever taken by the SBEC. Eventually, Vargas resigned.

My faith had been tested during this time, but later I found out that this experience was just a small bump in the road. However, Proverbs 3:5 says, "Trust in the Lord with all your heart and lean not on your own understanding." And I did.

25

A LARGER BUMP IN THE ROAD

This bump began one morning as I was taking a shower. I noticed a lump in my abdomen. The next morning, June 25, 2015, during an examination by my doctor, it took about ten seconds for him to look at my abdomen. He said, "I am referring you for a CT scan." Because of some scheduling conflicts, I went for the CT scan on Tuesday, June 30. Being inquisitive, I was curious what the doctor had seen, so I asked the technician. Her response was "It looks like lymphoma, but I can't be sure." *What?* I thought.

Then the doctor told me he would have the results for me by Friday. But nothing came on Friday or Saturday or Sunday. Nothing came on Monday, and now I was getting anxious and a little worried about this lymphoma thing. Finally, on July 7 I was informed that the diagnosis had been sent to my primary care doctor. Away I went to his office. My official diagnosis that day was "lymphadenopathy— mass lends itself to need a needle biopsy." Now that did not sound too good to me. My doctor agreed and said I must get it done in order to determine what would be the next step.

God must have been watching because I was able to schedule the needle biopsy the next day. The doctor was having trouble trying to determine where to insert the needle because he could not feel the lump that he had seen on the CT scan. He then asked the technician to use the sonogram to locate the "mass" to make sure he could get the samples he wanted. That poking around was a little uncomfortable.

By now I knew it could be a form of cancer, and I wanted to get these tests over because I wanted some answers.

On July 13 I received the needle biopsy report stating that I indeed had a form of cancer that required further tests in order to determine a treatment regimen.

Now my questions were turning to where could I get treatment and would my insurance cover my treatments. My quest began with frantic phone calls. First to MD Anderson in Houston, Texas, because my surgeon nephew was there being treated for lung cancer. After what seemed like an hour on the phone, I became frustrated and hung up. Next, I called Mayo Clinic in Phoenix, Arizona; and they would not accept my insurance. On I went to Lovelace Hospital in Albuquerque with the same results. Now I was down to the last place I could think of, the Presbyterian Hospital in Albuquerque, New Mexico. The most wonderful news came in less than ten minutes. The nurse said I would be admitted for testing and treatment. I would have a nurse navigator assigned, and all of my tests would be scheduled for me, as well as all of my appointments. *My goodness, what a blessing!*

The next day I received a call letting me know that I had been scheduled for a PET scan, a CT scan, and a bone morrow biopsy.

That bone morrow thing was more than uncomfortable. Now when I say "uncomfortable," I mean *ouch*! The doctor made three attempts to get an acceptable sample. When she said "You have strong bones," I thought that was a compliment. Then she turned to an intern who was observing and said, "Get the drill." I knew she really meant it.

Once I had completed these tests and had blood samples drawn, I was scheduled for my first oncologist's appointment on July 27 at 4:30 p.m. He did not waste any time getting to the point of my visit. With a big yellow pad (you know, just like the Big Chief tablets I had in grade school) in front of him, he was scribbling something as he looked at his computer. His words made it plain and were a little chilling: "Your cancer is *not curable* but *treatable*." He did not stop there. *Praise God.* He continued with options and outlined my alternatives. Then he read the following diagnosis to us: "Follicular B cell lymphoma, 90 percent diffuse on biopsy of mesenteric mass, low-grade histology; indolent lymphoma, stage 4, bone marrow involvement." That was a mouthful, and I still didn't understand exactly what he said. In fact, all I heard was "It is not curable but treatable." I now know what he said because he gave me the Big Chief paper from which he was reading.

Of course, my next question was when could I start treatment. Again, he got right to the point. He said first I must spend the next morning with an oncology nurse to make sure I understood what I would be experiencing. Then he gave us a few examples, ending with when he looked at my bald head and said, "Well, it doesn't look like you have to worry about losing your hair."

After we met with the nurse, she scared the daylights out of me. She said, "After you finish with a treatment, you will be your own worst enemy because you will not have an immune system. So stay away from crowds, avoid anyone who has any illness, and protect yourself. Otherwise, if you get sick during the treatments, you will have to start all over again." Because of that warning, I chose to basically isolate myself and remained at home, except for doctor visits, for the next seven months.

My first treatment began on August 3, 2015, and my last treatment was on December 21, 2015. These six months were filled with miracles. I was surrounded by more love than any one person deserves. Miracles were occurring on a daily basis. Think about it. Prayers began, and miracles started before I was officially diagnosed. I was at stage 4 with bone marrow involvement before I had any indication I even had a health issue. Prayers began with the first inclination that cancer might be a possibility. The first miracle was that the lymphoma growth must have already begun to shrink before the needle biopsy was taken. It took a sonogram to locate what my primary doctor had described as a large mass he had detected by just using his fingers.

The first morning I was to receive chemo, even before getting out of bed, my wife prayed that the chemo treatments would be like the living waters and healing streams from God. ("...he will lead them to springs of living water" (Revelation 7:17b, NIV). This continued each morning of treatment for the next six months. Believe me. That's exactly what God did!

The prayers and words of encouragement I received were very uplifting. I was thankful because I could use all of the encouragement I could get. During my treatments, friends and family from coast to coast were sending me cards and e-mails and praying for me. Because I had chosen to isolate myself, I was not expecting any visitors. Then one day a high school friend I had not seen in many years called. He and his wife had driven a couple of hundred miles to see me. So I reluctantly said yes but must have limited contact. He said they understood and came to the house.

During the conversation his wife, Carolyn, related to me that she also had been diagnosed with non-Hodgkin's lymphoma and she had been in remission for *ten years*. Now, that was a real piece of encouragement that no one else could give me. She gave me the gift of hope. They came to see me again the next year so we could all celebrate life together.

Unlike most cancer patients, I was blessed to have prisoners at two prison facilities praying for me because of my prior participation in the Kairos Prison Ministry.

My posttreatment recovery periods were a miracle in that they were "uneventful" compared to other chemo patients I had heard about. After I had completed my treatments, eventually I was able to return to participating in Kairos reunions (Saturday get-togethers for prayer). During one of these meetings, a participant asked me why I had not been attending the meetings. I told them about my cancer and treatments. Then they asked me if anything special had occurred. I went through the blessings and mentioned that I had received a prayer shawl from a church I had never attended. It was a real blessing because, when I got cold, it was a wonderful blessing to receive God's warmth packed in that prayer shawl.

Approximately one year later during a Kairos reunion, the fellows said they had crocheted 105 prayer shawls! They wanted to know if I could have them distributed to cancer patients and shut-ins. These shawls were dedicated on Sunday, November 18, 2017, and were distributed to shut-ins, cancer patients, nursing home patients, and others needing a touch of God's love during the 2017 Christmas season. Each one had a patch sewn on acknowledging that they were prepared by a Kairos brother.

I was so blessed to have angels masquerading as nurses, friends as supporters, strangers praying for me, and a wonderful dedicated wife to lift me up during every chemo treatment. While I still remain on a regular testing program, *I am a truly blessed man.*

IN THE UNITED STATES DISTRICT COURT
FOR THE WESTERN DISTRICT OF TEXAS
EL PASO DIVISION

ROBERT P. DURRETT, §
§
Plaintiff, §
§ Cause No. EP-99-CA-314-H
§
v. §
§
BOARD OF TRUSTEES FOR THE §
YSLETA INDEPENDENT SCHOOL §
DISTRICT and EDWARD LEE VARGAS, §
Individually, and in his capacity as §
SUPERINTENDENT, §
§
Defendants. §

Judgment

Before this Court is the notice of the parties that Defendants have offered judgment on the pleadings to Plaintiff pursuant to Rule 68 of the Federal Rules of Civil Procedure in the amount of $. Plaintiff has accepted the offer pursuant to Rule 68 in a timely manner.

Accordingly, it is ORDERED, ADJUDGED AND DECREED that Judgment is entered for Plaintiff in the amount of $ and that this sum includes all costs, fees, expenses incurred by the Plaintiff.

SIGNED AND ENTERED, this the 21st day of May, 2001.

_____
Harry Lee Hudspeth
U.S. District Judge

-1-

Judge's final order

Last chemo treatment complete! Celebrated
with banging the gong.

The Prayer Shawl came to me from a
church I had never attended.

The youth group of my church sent me this get-well card. The letters are formed by the youth using their bodies to form the letters.

DEPOSITIONS

Oral deposition of Robert Duane Durrett
January 19, 2000

Oral deposition of Edward Lee Vargas
January 18 and 19, 2000

Oral deposition of Charles William Peartree
February 8, 2000

Oral deposition of Ronda C. Scrivner
January 5, 2000

Oral deposition of "the teacher"
February 8, 2000

Written depositions of Jacqueline Strashun
April 3, 2000

Ysleta Independent School District vs. Antonio Trujillo
Opinion of the hearing examiner, Juergen Koetter
December 9, 1998

Edward Lee Vargas Affidavit
November 10, 1999

ABOUT THE AUTHOR

For over thirty-five years, Robert Durrett's major employment emphasis was on human resources management. The whistle-blower complaint he filed led to his unlawful termination.

He was born in a dentist's office in a small town in eastern New Mexico. He was reared in Portales, New Mexico, where he attended public schools. He graduated from Eastern New Mexico University (ENMU) with a BA in Business Administration and Finance, an MBA in Marketing, and an Educational Specialist degree. He also received a Doctorate in Education from Texas Tech University.

His career included stints in banking, retailing, and education. In education he served as director of community services, assistant to the president, and personnel director at ENMU. He also served as personnel director and assistant vice president for administrative and human resources services at the University of Texas in El Paso. His last positions in education were associate superintendent for human resources and interim superintendent at Ysleta Independent School District, El Paso, Texas.

His varied background included being elected to two terms as a city councilman. His volunteer involvement included being assistant scoutmaster of Troop 18, member of the Conquistador Council of the BSA, and assistant scoutmaster for the council's National Jamboree Troop T-780 in 1981. Other activities included the Kiwanis Club and the College and University Personnel Association.

His major focus as a volunteer for the past twenty-five years has been his participation in Kairos Prison Ministry programs. He participated in Kairos programs at La Tuna Federal Prison in Texas and New Mexico prisons in Santa Fe Prison, Southern New Mexico Correctional Facility, Otero County Prison Facility, and Guadalupe County Prison Facility.